365 Days of Stitch

Keep a personal embr
motifs, techniques

STEPH ARNOLD

Search Press

A QUARTO BOOK

Published in 2023 by
Search Press Limited
Wellwood, North Farm Road,
Tunbridge Wells, Kent TN2 3DR

Copyright © 2023 Quarto Publishing plc

All rights reserved. No part of this publication may be reproduced, stored in a retrieval system or transmitted in any form by any means, electronic, mechanical, photocopying, recording or otherwise, without the permission of the copyright owner.

ISBN: 978-1-80092-226-6
ebook ISBN: 978-1-80093-208-1

Extra copies of the templates are available from:
www.bookmarkedhub.com

This book was conceived, edited and designed by Quarto Publishing, an imprint of Quarto
1 Triptych Place
London SE1 9SH
www.quarto.com

QUAR.421446

Editor: Charlene Fernandes
Editorial Assistant: Elinor Ward
Designer: Sally Bond
Photographer: Nicki Dowey
Senior Art Editor: Rachel Cross
Deputy Art Director: Martina Calvio
Managing Director: Lesley Henderson
Publisher: Lorraine Dickey

Illustrations © Steph Arnold (pp 16–21)

Printed in China

Bookmarked Hub
For further ideas and inspiration, and to join our free online community, visit
www.bookmarkedhub.com

Contents

Meet Steph	4	HOME	44	PERSONAL CARE	96
About this Book	5	Houseplants	44	Beauty	96
Artists' Samplers	6	Home Improvement	46	Clothes	98
		Cooking	48	Shoes and Accessories	100

CHAPTER 1:
Core Techniques and Stitches — 10

BEFORE YOU START

Tools and materials	12
How to fit the fabric to the hoop	13
Colours	13
Templates	14
Transferring the motif to the fabric	15
How to finish the back of the hoop	15

STITCHES — 16

CHAPTER 2:
Motif Directory — 22

ANIMALS — 24

On the Farm	24
Reptiles and Dinosaurs	26
Zoo Animals	28
Birds	30
Insects	32
Pets	34
Sea Life	36

NATURE — 38

Plants and Fungi	38
Flowers	40
Weather	42

FOOD AND DRINK — 50

Food	50
More Food	52
Fruit and Veg	54
Drinks	56
Sweet Treats	58
Sweets	60

CELEBRATIONS — 62

Wedding	62
Easter	64
Birthday	66
Valentine's Day	68
Halloween	70
Christmas	72
Religions and Celebrations	74

WORK AND PLAY — 76

Travel	76
Ball Sports	78
Other Sports	80
Hobbies	82
More Hobbies	84
Music	86
The Great Outdoors	88
At the Beach	90
Entertainment	92
Work and Education	94

CHILDREN — 102

Baby	102
Toys	104

MIND, BODY AND SPIRIT — 106

Spiritual	106
Astrology	108
Health	110

ASTRONOMY — 112

Space	112

GENRE — 114

Fantasy	114

COMMUNICATION — 116

Symbols	116
Doodles	118
Emojis	120
Alphabets, Numbers and Diacritics	122

Index	124
Acknowledgements	128

MEET STEPH

Meet Steph

Hi, I'm Steph!

I started embroidery over 10 years ago after facing struggles with my mental health. I found it a great way to distract from ruminating thoughts, de-stress and feel a real sense of achievement once a piece was complete. It combined my love of designing and crafting, and I was hooked after the first stitch.

After a few years teaching myself various stitches and working on patterns, I put my Product Design degree to good use and launched my embroidery kit business Oh Sew Bootiful so that I could pass on the joy of needlecraft in the hope that it might help others who were having similar struggles.

I'm now a mum to two boys, and my husband and one of my best friends have joined the business – I can't quite believe that I get to design and craft for a living with the people I love the most.

Even though my spare time is more scarce now, I love nothing more than curling up on the sofa to get my stitch on with a good scary movie playing in the background!

I've found thread journalling a great way to be mindful, looking out for the positives in each day (no matter how small) while practising and broadening my embroidery skills. I really hope you find this book helps you to do the same!

About this Book

Embroidery journalling is a great way to focus on the positives of each day, no matter how small. It could be something as little as eating your favourite chocolate bar or catching up on a good TV series while also highlighting the bigger life events! By stitching a motif each day, you'll be able to look back on your year and the finished hoop as both a lovely keepsake and a personal journal.

HOW TO USE THIS BOOK

You can use this book to help decide what to stitch by flicking through for inspiration or by going to the most relevant category (use the contents or the index). Once you've decided on a motif, you can either copy it to your fabric or use it as reference to make the design more personal. We've included colours and stitch suggestions as reference but feel free to customise the motifs how you wish! If it's your first time making a thread journal, I would recommend using cotton fabric in an embroidery hoop as it's easy to manage and you can use the whole working area. There is nothing to stop you using these motifs for other projects. You could, for example, decorate a canvas make-up bag with some of the make-up icons, or add some cookery icons to an apron or some of the flowers to a pair of gardening gloves.

THE MOTIFS

The motifs in this book are all scaled to approximately 14mm (½in), which means you can fit 365 on a 30.5cm (12in) hoop. Some people also find that using an M&M sweet can be helpful in sizing motifs but bear in mind that some motifs will naturally be longer, thinner, taller and more detailed than others, so don't worry about making them all exactly the same size. You can always scale simpler motifs to be smaller and adjust the sizing to work with the space you have as you go along.

MONTHS OF THE YEAR

To customise your hoop, you can try stitching the months of the year in each segment and include the year so you can look back on it in the future. There's a section at the back with lettering and numbers to help if needed.

GETTING STARTED

There are no hard-and-fast rules when it comes to this project. You're creating your thread journal for yourself, so feel free to stitch as often or as little as you like. It can help to keep a list of the motifs you'd like to stitch in case you don't get a chance to stitch every single day. Some people just stitch when something particularly good has happened or just a few larger motifs to show the highlights of each month. Your journal, your rules!

Don't feel pressure for each design to be perfect. Once you've got a few motifs down, your eye will be drawn to the piece as a whole and won't focus on any minute flaws there may be! This should be a project that you enjoy stitching, whether that's by keeping the designs really simple as a way to remember your year, experimenting with more complex stitches, or adding beads and wire to expand your skills!

ARTISTS' SAMPLERS

Artists' Samplers

Check out the thread journals by these embroidery artists. Each one looks different, which shows you can really put your own spin on a hoop and personalise it in your own style.

Jessica McCloy

Threads and embellishments: DMC embroidery floss, glass beads, found objects (a tiny shell)

Fabric and hoop: linen blend fabric, in a 30.5cm (12in) hoop, high-thread cotton

Stitches: Satin Stitch, Back Stitch, French Knot, Fishbone Stitch, Turkey Work Stitch, beads

Strawberry
page 54

'Some days I had more time to spend on embroidery, and on others life got in the way and I'd go a week or so without doing it, but I'd try to make a note of missed days so that when I was able to catch up, I'd know where I was at. I had a huge list on my phone where I wrote my embroidery plan for each day of the year, sometimes with a little reminder to myself of why I had chosen a particular motif.'

Follow Jessica on Instagram @marisko_stitches.

Flamingo
page 30

Pumpkin page 70

Butterfly page 32

'I have been creating thread journals since 2019 and will continue to do so for the rest of my life. This hoop covers births, deaths, global pandemics and everything in between. I use photographs on my phone to keep track of my stitches – this can double up as a reference as well as a reminder. This 2020 thread journal is my favourite, as it contains the entire timeline of the arrival of my second daughter, from when we first found out I was pregnant, to scans (towards the bottom of the hoop), heartbeat and birth (her name, Nancy).'

Stephanie Evans

Threads and embellishments: DMC embroidery floss, glass beads, appliquéd items (corner of a tea bag)

Fabric and hoop: 100 per cent cotton, thick drill fabric, in a 20cm (8in) embroidery hoop

Stitches: Back Stitch, Whipped Back Stitch, Satin Stitch, French Knot, Colonial Knot, Fishbone Stitch, Turkey Work Stitch, Stump Work, Lazy Daisy, Long and Short Stitch (thread painting), Fly Stitch, Bullion Knot, seed beads

Follow Stephanie on Instagram and TikTok @evanssentcreations or join her Facebook group 'Thread Journal Club' to share your journey in thread journalling.

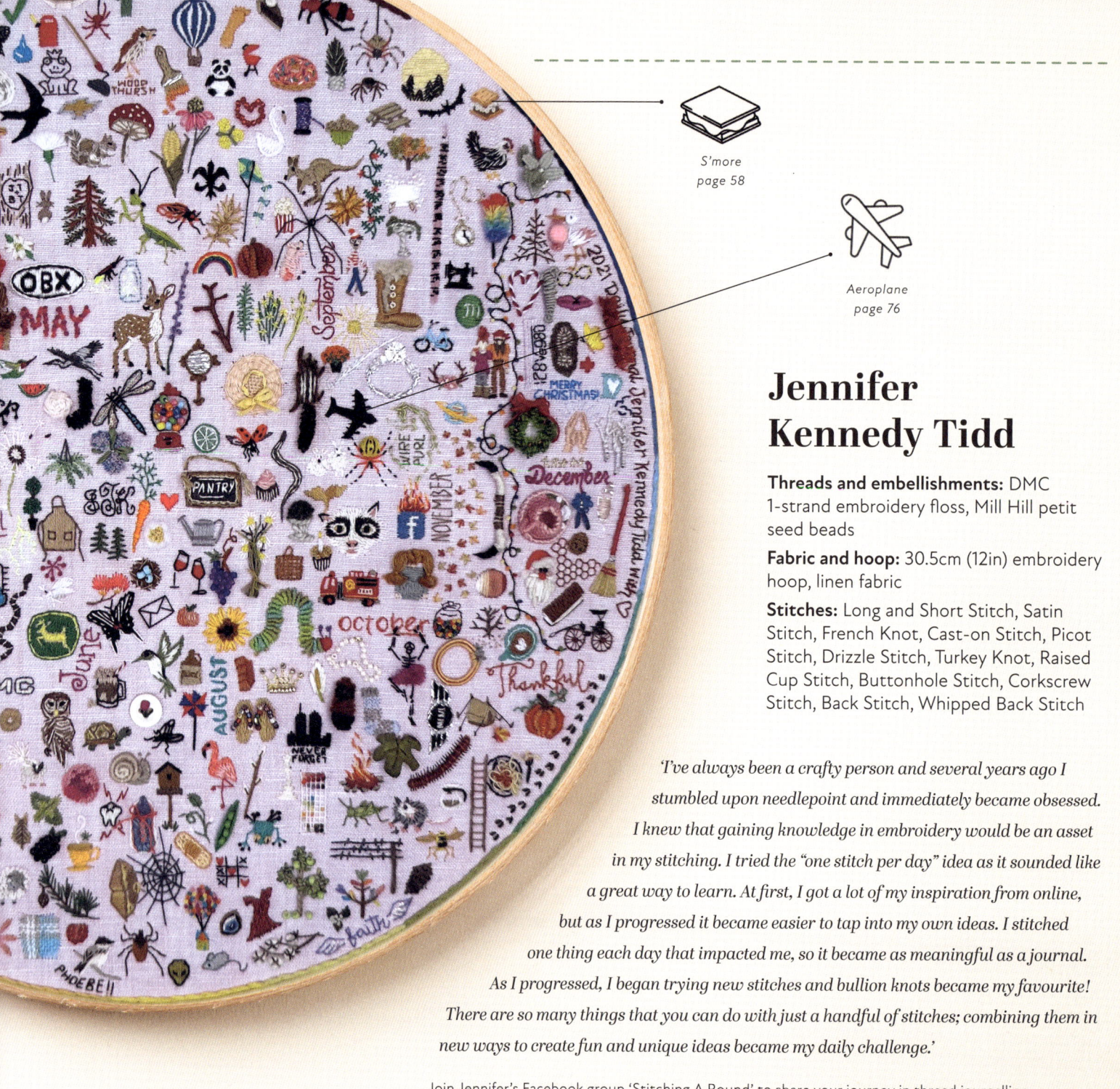

S'more
page 58

Aeroplane
page 76

Jennifer Kennedy Tidd

Threads and embellishments: DMC 1-strand embroidery floss, Mill Hill petit seed beads

Fabric and hoop: 30.5cm (12in) embroidery hoop, linen fabric

Stitches: Long and Short Stitch, Satin Stitch, French Knot, Cast-on Stitch, Picot Stitch, Drizzle Stitch, Turkey Knot, Raised Cup Stitch, Buttonhole Stitch, Corkscrew Stitch, Back Stitch, Whipped Back Stitch

'I've always been a crafty person and several years ago I stumbled upon needlepoint and immediately became obsessed. I knew that gaining knowledge in embroidery would be an asset in my stitching. I tried the "one stitch per day" idea as it sounded like a great way to learn. At first, I got a lot of my inspiration from online, but as I progressed it became easier to tap into my own ideas. I stitched one thing each day that impacted me, so it became as meaningful as a journal. As I progressed, I began trying new stitches and bullion knots became my favourite! There are so many things that you can do with just a handful of stitches; combining them in new ways to create fun and unique ideas became my daily challenge.'

Join Jennifer's Facebook group 'Stitching A Round' to share your journey in thread journalling.

ARTISTS' SAMPLERS

Sophie O'Neill

Threads and embellishments: DMC 6-strand embroidery floss, DMC Gold Light Effects thread
Fabric and hoop: 30.5cm (12in) embroidery hoop, Kona 100 per cent cotton fabric
Stitches: Back Stitch, Lazy Daisy, Chain Stitch, Satin Stitch, Whipped Back Stitch, Long and Short Stitch, French Knot

'I first started teaching myself to embroider in 2019 and started my first embroidery journal back in 2020. I was starting a brand new job and thought it would be a fun way to document my year; but, it all went awry once I was furloughed due to the pandemic. However, I never managed to run out of things to add to my embroidery journal; there was always something unique to do, even when you're stuck in your home. Since then, my embroidery journals have documented an international move to Scotland, multiple different jobs, starting my embroidery business and even more memorable moments ...'

Follow Sophie on Instagram and TikTok @thestircrazycrafter.

Pizza page 52

Candy Corn page 70

CHAPTER 1:

Core Techniques and Stitches

Learn what tools and materials you will need as well as how to fit the fabric to the hoop and get started. There are also step-by-step instructions for the 15 stitches included in this chapter which you can refer back to after picking each day's motif.

CORE TECHNIQUES AND STITCHES

Before You Start

Before you dive in, you will need to purchase a few tools and materials. I have listed the most useful as well as a few optional supplies below. You can then use a journal template if you wish (see page 14) and get started!

Tools and materials

ESSENTIAL

1. **Embroidery needles** As we'll only be working with one or two strands of embroidery thread, a size 7 needle works well.
2. **Embroidery threads** We've used DMC embroidery floss for this book but feel free to use your favourite brand.
3. **Embroidery hoop** The motifs in this book are designed to fit a 30.5cm (12in) hoop (see opposite). I prefer the wooden ones as they hold the fabric taut and are nice to work with, but there are lots of other options out there!
4. **Heat erasable pen** for sketching out your designs.
5. **Iron** to smooth out the fabric and to transfer the template if using (not shown).
6. **Coloured or white cotton fabric** – 100 per cent cotton is best as it's a fine weave and doesn't stretch out of shape when put in the hoop.
7. **Scissors or thread cutter**
8. **Polycotton thread** to finish the back of the hoop. We've used DMC here.
9. **Pinking shears** for cutting out the fabric.

OPTIONAL

10. Pin cushion
11. Needle threader
12. Stitch unpicker
13. Needle minder
14. Wires, beads, ribbon, wool, sequins

SPLITTING THE THREADS

Embroidery threads are made up of six strands. Due to the tiny nature of the motifs in the book, you'll want to work with one or two of these strands. To split them, simply cut a length of thread (a forearm's length works well), then pull out the individual strand(s) before threading the needle.

How to fit the fabric to the hoop

1. Unscrew the embroidery hoop. You will now have two parts: the inner and the outer hoop.
2. Place the inner hoop on a flat surface such as a table.
3. Lay the fabric over the top of the inner hoop, making sure it's as flat as possible.
4. Then place the outer hoop over the top and press down, sandwiching the fabric in between.
5. Go around the edge of the hoop, pulling the fabric taut while tightening the screw of the hoop to secure it all in place.
6. The fabric should be tight in the hoop, without any pulling. If it is too baggy, it can lead to problems when you start stitching.

If you find the fabric becomes looser as you stitch, you can repeat steps 5–6.

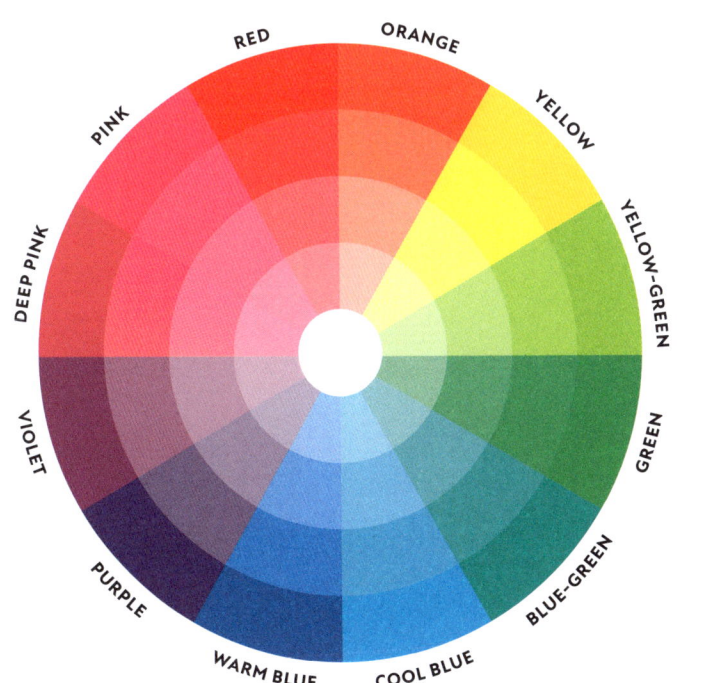

Colours

You can follow the DMC colour suggestions provided with each motif or you can choose your own. Sometimes colours for motifs will be obvious to you, so just go with what you think. If you're struggling to choose colours that complement each other then use this colour wheel to help. As a rule of thumb, any colours opposite each other on the colour wheel work well together. For example, Yellow and Purple, Green and Orange, and Red and Blue pair really nicely together.

13

CORE TECHNIQUES AND STITCHES

Templates

Transferring a design from template to fabric is the first step in completing an embroidery piece. You can draw the design onto the fabric by hand, or iron the design directly onto the fabric using the transfer sheets provided (marked with an iron icon).

HOW TO USE AN IRON-ON TEMPLATE

1 Position the template on top of the fabric, making sure it's central.
2 Gently press the iron on top of the transfer and fabric, moving it across the whole template.
3 It can take up to 10 seconds for the design to transfer, so make sure that all areas are covered.
4 To check that the design has transferred, gently lift a corner to make sure before removing the template completely.

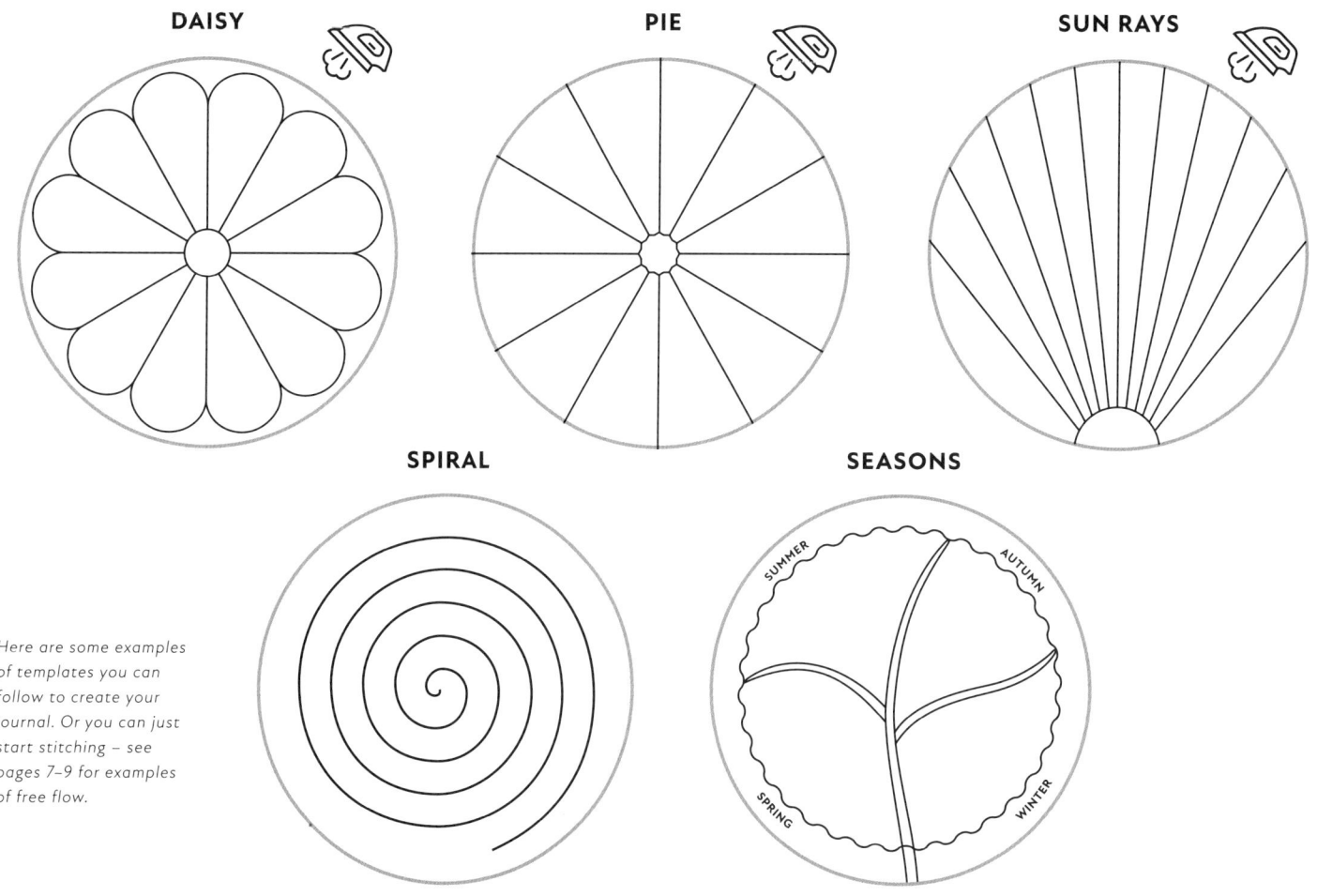

Here are some examples of templates you can follow to create your journal. Or you can just start stitching – see pages 7–9 for examples of free flow.

BEFORE YOU START

Transferring the motif to the fabric

We recommend using the motifs in this book as reference to draw your own version on the fabric. Heat erasable pens work really well on fabric and the ink can easily be removed with a blast of a blow dryer once you've finished stitching a motif or to correct any errors when you're drawing.

If you'd prefer to trace the motifs, you may find it helpful to trace them onto tracing paper or photocopy them before transferring them to the fabric. If you use this method, you'll need a light source such as a window or lightbox to see the image through the fabric.

How to finish the back of the hoop

Once your thread journal is stitched, you can finish the back of the hoop to make it look more presentable. Then you can display it on a wall or shelf.

1. Cut back the fabric into a circle, leaving at least 2.5cm all the way around the edge of the hoop. It's best to use pinking shears for this to prevent the fabric fraying.
2. Thread a needle with polycotton thread, at least twice the circumference of the hoop.
3. Tie a knot in the end of the thread and make a running stitch all the way around the edge of the fabric.
4. Once you get back around to where you started, pull both ends of the thread to gather the fabric behind the hoop.
5. Tie the two ends of the thread together a couple of times to secure, then snip off the ends.

CORE TECHNIQUES AND STITCHES

Stitches

There are step-by-step instructions for 15 stitches included in this chapter, which you can refer back to after picking each day's motif. You don't need to stick to the suggested stitches for each motif and you could try mixing them up by switching different outline stitches, such as Back Stitch, Stem Stitch or Split Stitch, and different filling stitches like French knots and Satin Stitch.

STARTING A KNOT
1. Using one end of the thread, create a loop and tuck the end of the thread through the loop.
2. Pull the thread through tightly, to create the knot. Repeat to secure if necessary.

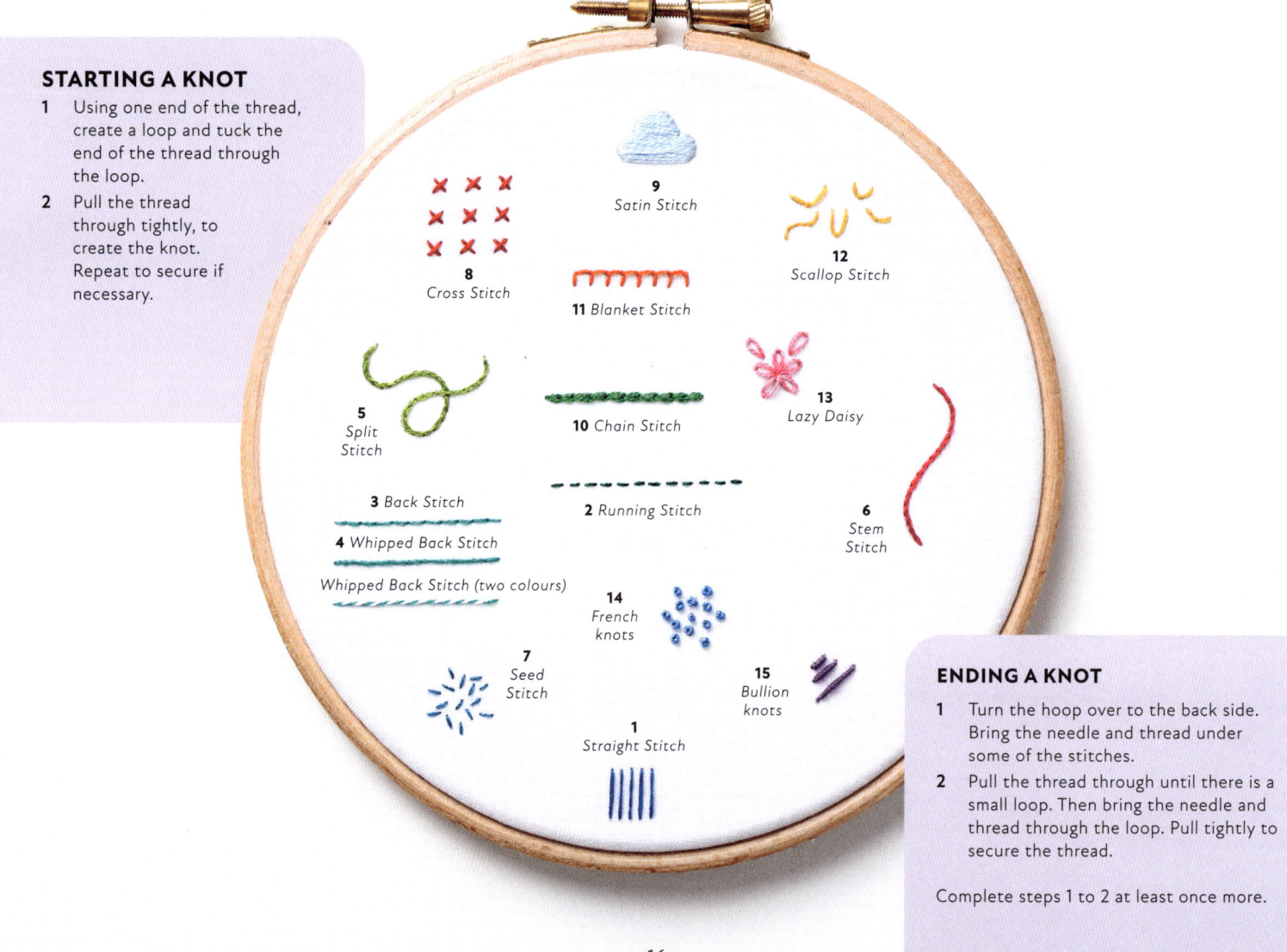

ENDING A KNOT
1. Turn the hoop over to the back side. Bring the needle and thread under some of the stitches.
2. Pull the thread through until there is a small loop. Then bring the needle and thread through the loop. Pull tightly to secure the thread.

Complete steps 1 to 2 at least once more.

STITCHES

1 STRAIGHT STITCH ──────

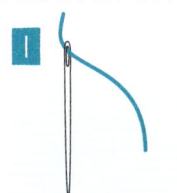  

Push the needle up through the fabric and then back down at the desired length of the stitch.

This is the basis for many of the stitches you'll find in embroidery.

Here are a couple of examples of how you can create a variety of patterns with this simple stitch.

3D STITCHES
You can get really technical with your motifs by making them three-dimensional and textured as Jennifer has with her hoop (see page 8). You can even try incorporating other types of materials into your thread journal such as ribbon, beads, yarn, sequins or wire. The possibilities here are endless!

2 RUNNING STITCH ─ ─ ─ ─ ─

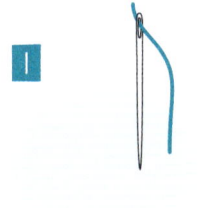  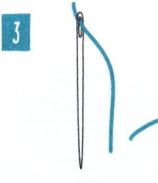 

Push the needle up through the fabric and then back down a short distance away.

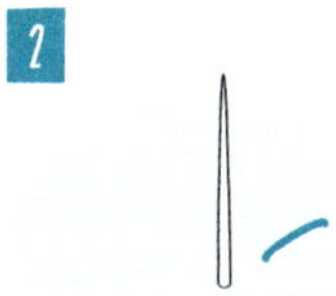

Push the needle back up through the fabric, leaving a small gap.

Push the needle back down through the fabric to create a second stitch.

Continue this technique to produce a row of running stitches.

3 BACK STITCH ─ ─ ─ ─ ─

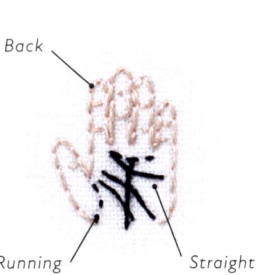

Back
Running *Straight*

Palm Reading
page 106

  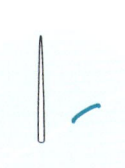  

Push the needle up through the fabric and then back down a short distance away.

Push the needle back up through the fabric, double the length of your original stitch.

Push the needle back down through the fabric at the end of your original stitch.

Continue this technique to produce a row of back stitches.

CORE TECHNIQUES AND STITCHES

4 WHIPPED BACK STITCH

Yin Yang
page 106

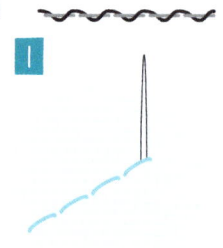
1 Complete Back Stitch as required, then push the needle up through the fabric at the beginning of the Back Stitch line.

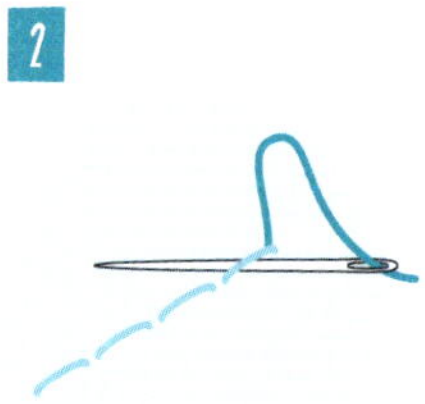

2 Use the needle to 'whip' under each stitch, avoiding going through the fabric.

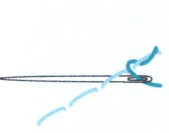
3 Bring the needle back to the other side of the stitch and repeat steps 2 and 3.

4 Always go under each Back Stitch from the same side to avoid 'lacing' rather than 'whipping' the back stitches.

5 SPLIT STITCH

Bacon
page 50

1 Push the needle up through the fabric and then back down a short distance away to create a stitch.

2 Push the needle back up through the fabric between the strands of the first stitch, splitting the thread in half.

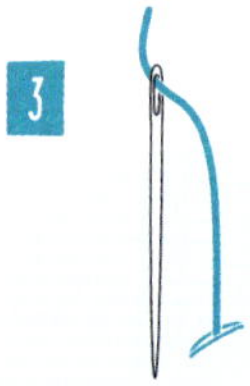

3 Pull the needle down to create a stitch.

4 Continue this technique to produce a row of split stitches.

6 STEM STITCH

Lemon
page 54

1 Push the needle up through the fabric and create a stitch on a slight angle from the direction you're moving.

2 Push the needle back up through the fabric next to the stitch, along the direction you are stitching, and create a stitch.

3 Continue this technique to produce a row of stem stitches.

STITCHES

7 SEED STITCH

Strawberry
page 54

1 Push the needle up through the fabric and then back down at the desired length of the stitch.

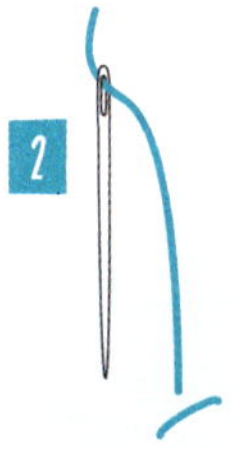

2 Push the needle back up through the fabric a short distance away and then back down to create a second stitch.

Repeat this process and build up a group of random seed stitches to create the desired effect.

It's up to you how random or uniform you want your stitches to be.

8 CROSS STITCH

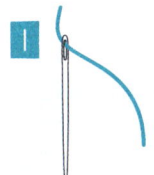

Cross stitch
page 82

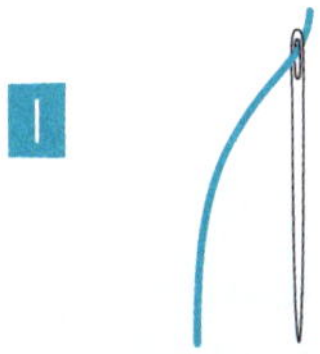

1 Push the needle up through the fabric and create a diagonal stitch.

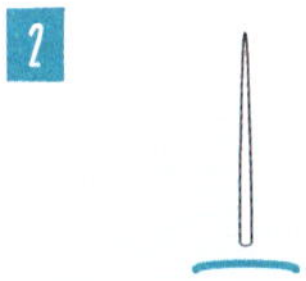

2 Push the needle back up through the fabric in line (horizontally and vertically) with both points of your original stitch.

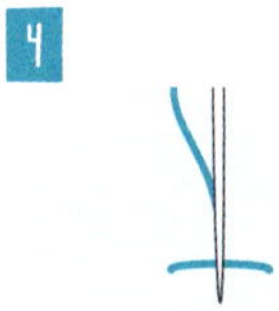

4 Push the needle back down through the fabric, crossing your original stitch.

5 This creates your first Cross Stitch. Continue this technique to produce the required pattern in your design.

9 SATIN STITCH

Moon and Star
page 118

1 Push the needle up through the fabric and then back down to create a Straight Stitch.

2 Push the needle up through the fabric next to where you started your first stitch.

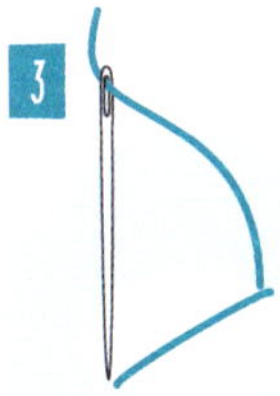

3 Push the needle back down through the fabric on the outline of the shape you wish to fill, creating a second Straight Stitch.

4 Repeat this process to fill the shape.

19

CORE TECHNIQUES AND STITCHES

10 CHAIN STITCH

Sweater
page 98

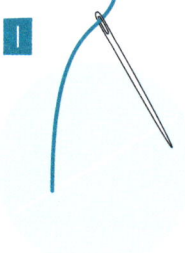

1 Push the needle up through the fabric.

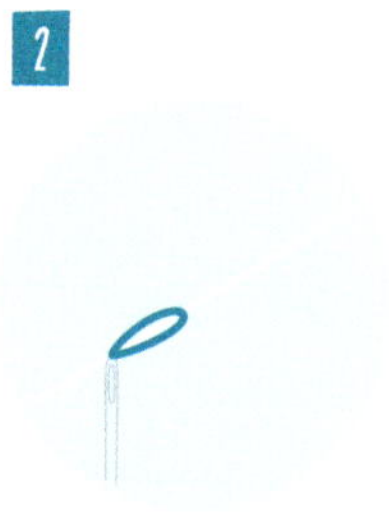

2 Pull the needle down through the hole you just came up, leaving a loop on top of the fabric.

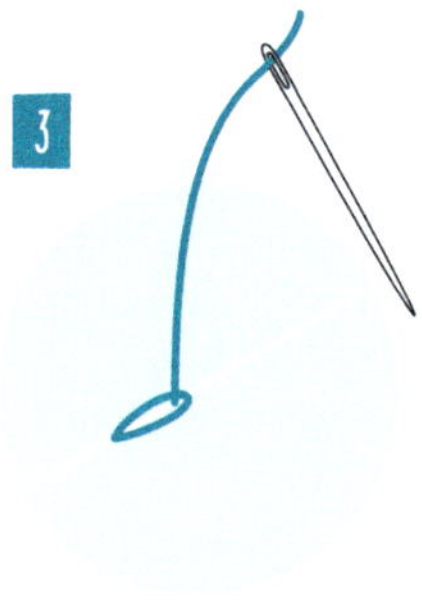

3 Pull the needle down through the hole you just came up, leaving a second loop on top of the fabric.

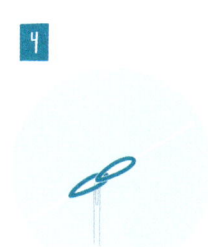

4 Push the needle up through the fabric a stitch length apart. Repeat steps 3 and 4 to create a row of chains.

11 BLANKET STITCH

Banana
page 60

1 Push the needle up through the fabric and create a diagonal stitch.

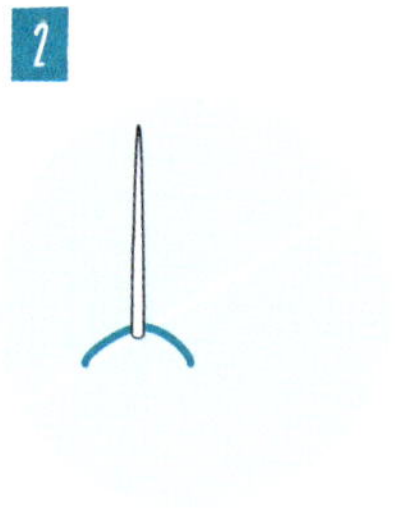

2 Push the needle back up, creating a right angle in the diagonal stitch. Catch the thread and pull it taut.

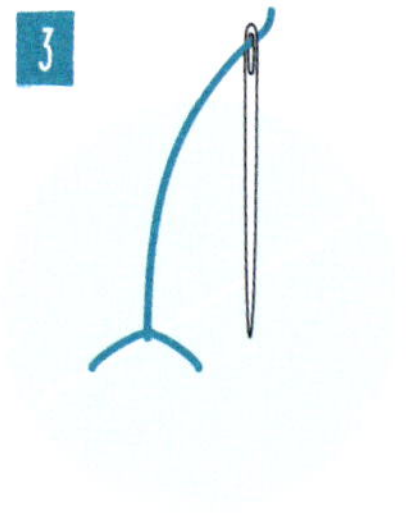

3 Create another diagonal stitch.

4 Repeat the process to create a row of blanket stitches.

12 SCALLOP STITCH

Gymnastics
page 80

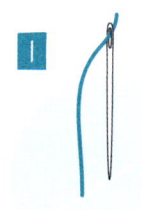

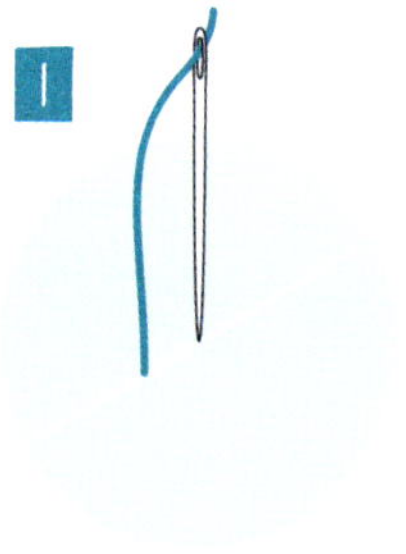

1 Push the needle up through the fabric and pull the thread all the way through.

2 Pull the needle down through the fabric, creating a loose stitch.

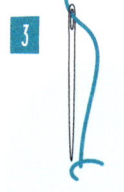

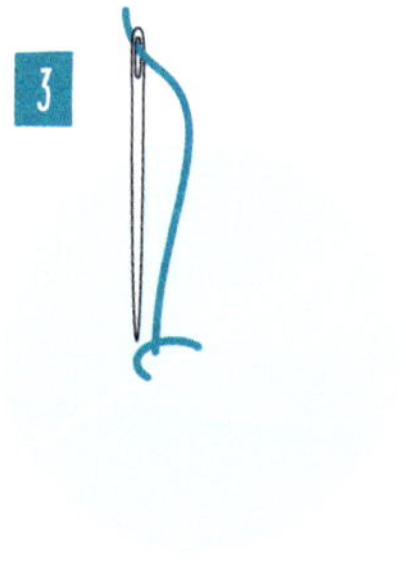

3 Push the needle up through the fabric a small space away and catch the loop with the needle. Pull the thread through so that the loop is taut.

4 Anchor the loop with a small stitch and repeat. Start the next stitch at the end of the original stitch.

STITCHES

13 LAZY DAISY

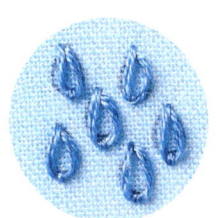

Raindrops
page 42

1 Push the needle up through the fabric and pull the thread all the way through.

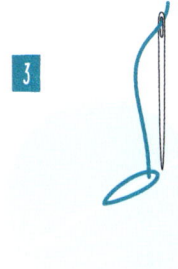

2 Pull the needle down through the same hole, leaving a loop on top of the fabric.

3 Push the needle up through the fabric a small space away and catch the loop with the needle. Pull taut and anchor the loop with a small stitch.

4 Repeat this process around the centre point to create a daisy.

14 FRENCH KNOT

Gumball Machine
page 60

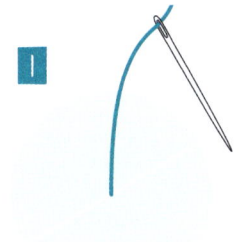

1 Push the needle up through the fabric.

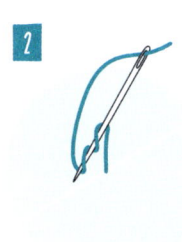

2 With the needle close to the fabric, wrap the thread around the needle two or three times.

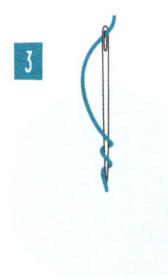

3 Holding the thread taut, pull the needle down through the hole you just came up.

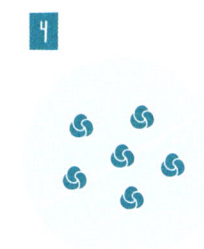

4 You should be left with a small, round knot.

15 BULLION KNOT

Campfire
page 88

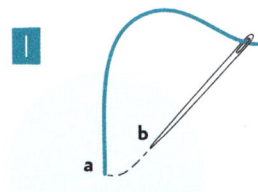

1 Push the needle up through the fabric (a) and then back down a short distance away (b).

2 Push the needle up through the original hole and wrap the thread around the needle a number of times, as desired.

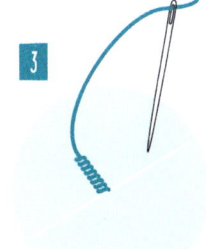

3 Use your free hand to hold the stitches in place, then pull the needle all the way through.

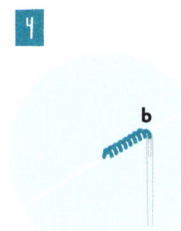

4 Push the needle down through hole (b) to complete the stitch.

21

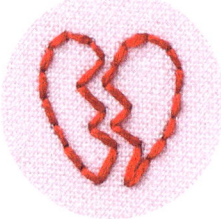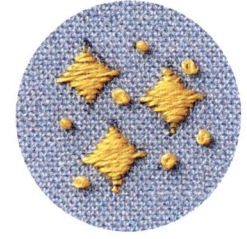

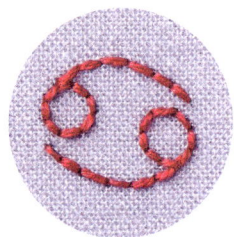

CHAPTER 2:

Motif Directory

Here you'll find 1,000 motifs for you to use or to inspire the designs for your thread journal. They're split into 50 categories to make it easier for you to find what you're looking for. Feel free to copy them directly or put your own twist on them. You can use the colours (DMC codes provided) and stitches suggested or get experimental with your own!

ANIMALS

On the Farm

COLOURS

Yellow 972
Peach 754
Orange 946
Red 321
Burgundy 814
Deep pink 600
Pink 603
Lilac 554
Purple 552
Deep blue 798
Blue 334
Pale blue 3841
Teal 3809
Green 701
Moss green 581
Dark green 3818
Brown 898
Tan 167
Beige 739
Grey 414
White BLANC
Black 310

Tractor
Red, Black, Grey
Straight Stitch, Scallop Stitch, Satin Stitch

Barn
Red, Brown
Straight Stitch, Scallop Stitch

Wheat
Tan
Straight Stitch, Scallop Stitch

Scarecrow
Tan, Beige, Brown
Scallop Stitch, Straight Stitch, Back Stitch

Chicken
Red, Beige, Yellow, Black
Scallop Stitch, Back Stitch, French Knot

Cow Face
Brown, Beige, Tan, Black
Back Stitch, Satin Stitch, French Knot, Scallop Stitch

Bull Face
Black, Brown, Yellow, Beige
Stem Stitch, Split Stitch, Scallop Stitch, French Knot

Sheep Face
Tan, Beige, Black
French Knot, Scallop Stitch, Seed Stitch

Pig Face
Pink, Black
Back Stitch, Scallop Stitch, French Knot

Goat Face
Beige, Tan, Black
French Knot, Scallop Stitch, Back Stitch

Horse Face
Brown, Black, Tan
French Knot, Scallop Stitch, Satin Stitch

Bag of Wheat
Tan
Stem Stitch, Scallop Stitch, Straight Stitch

Farmer's Hat
Tan, Red
Satin Stitch

Fields
Yellow, Purple, Moss green, Brown
Satin Stitch, Straight Stitch, Split Stitch

Pig
Pink
Scallop Stitch, Back Stitch

Lamb
Beige, Black
Scallop Stitch, Split Stitch, French Knot

Sheep
Tan, Beige, Black
French Knot, Satin Stitch, Seed Stitch

Goose
White, Yellow, Black
Back Stitch, Scallop Stitch, Seed Stitch

Cow
Brown, Tan, Black, Pink
Scallop Stitch, Satin Stitch, Back Stitch, Straight Stitch

Horse
Tan, Brown, Black
Scallop Stitch, Satin Stitch, Seed Stitch, Straight Stitch

'French knots add so much texture and are perfect for the sheep's wool. If you're a bit unsure of them, you could easily switch them out for another stitch such as Chain or Satin.'

ANIMALS

Reptiles and Dinosaurs

COLOURS

Yellow 972
Peach 754
Orange 946
Red 321
Burgundy 814
Deep pink 600
Pink 603
Lilac 554
Purple 552
Deep blue 798
Blue 334
Pale blue 3841
Teal 3809
Green 701
Moss green 581
Dark green 3818
Brown 898
Tan 167
Beige 739
Grey 414
White BLANC
Black 310

Snake
Moss green, Red
Split Stitch, Satin Stitch, Straight Stitch

Gecko
Green
Satin Stitch, Straight Stitch

Cobra
Green, Red, Tan
Straight Stitch, Scallop Stitch, Blanket Stitch

Chameleon
Teal
French Knot, Back Stitch, Scallop Stitch

Lizard
Dark green, Black
Satin Stitch, French Knot, Straight Stitch

Striped Lizard
Orange, Yellow, Black
Satin Stitch, Scallop Stitch, French Knot

Tortoise
Moss green, Tan, Brown
Satin Stitch, Split Stitch, Back Stitch

Crocodile
Green, Dark green, Black
Scallop Stitch, Back Stitch, French Knot

Rattlesnake
Tan, Brown, Red, Black
Scallop Stitch, Back Stitch, Straight Stitch

Hatching Egg
Beige, Red, Dark green
Whipped Back Stitch, Back Stitch, Straight Stitch, Scallop Stitch

T-Rex
Brown, White, Black
Scallop Stitch, Stem Stitch, French Knot

Stegosaurus
Dark green, Tan
Back Stitch, Scallop Stitch, Straight Stitch

Triceratops
Tan, Black, Beige
Straight Stitch, Scallop Stitch, Back Stitch, French Knot

Brontosaurus
Grey
Scallop Stitch

Pterodactyl
Grey, Black, Orange
Satin Stitch, Stem Stitch, French Knot

Footprints
Brown
Satin Stitch

Komodo Dragon
Brown, Tan, Black
Straight Stitch, Scallop Stitch, French Knot

Tree Frog
Moss green, Red, Black, Beige
Scallop Stitch, Back Stitch, Satin Stitch

Toad
Tan, Brown
Back Stitch, Scallop Stitch, Seed Stitch, French Knot

Alligator
Dark green, Beige, Tan
Back Stitch, Scallop Stitch, French Knot

'The bottom edge of the tortoise's shell is stitched with Split Stitch. You could stitch this in a contrasting colour to make it stand out.'

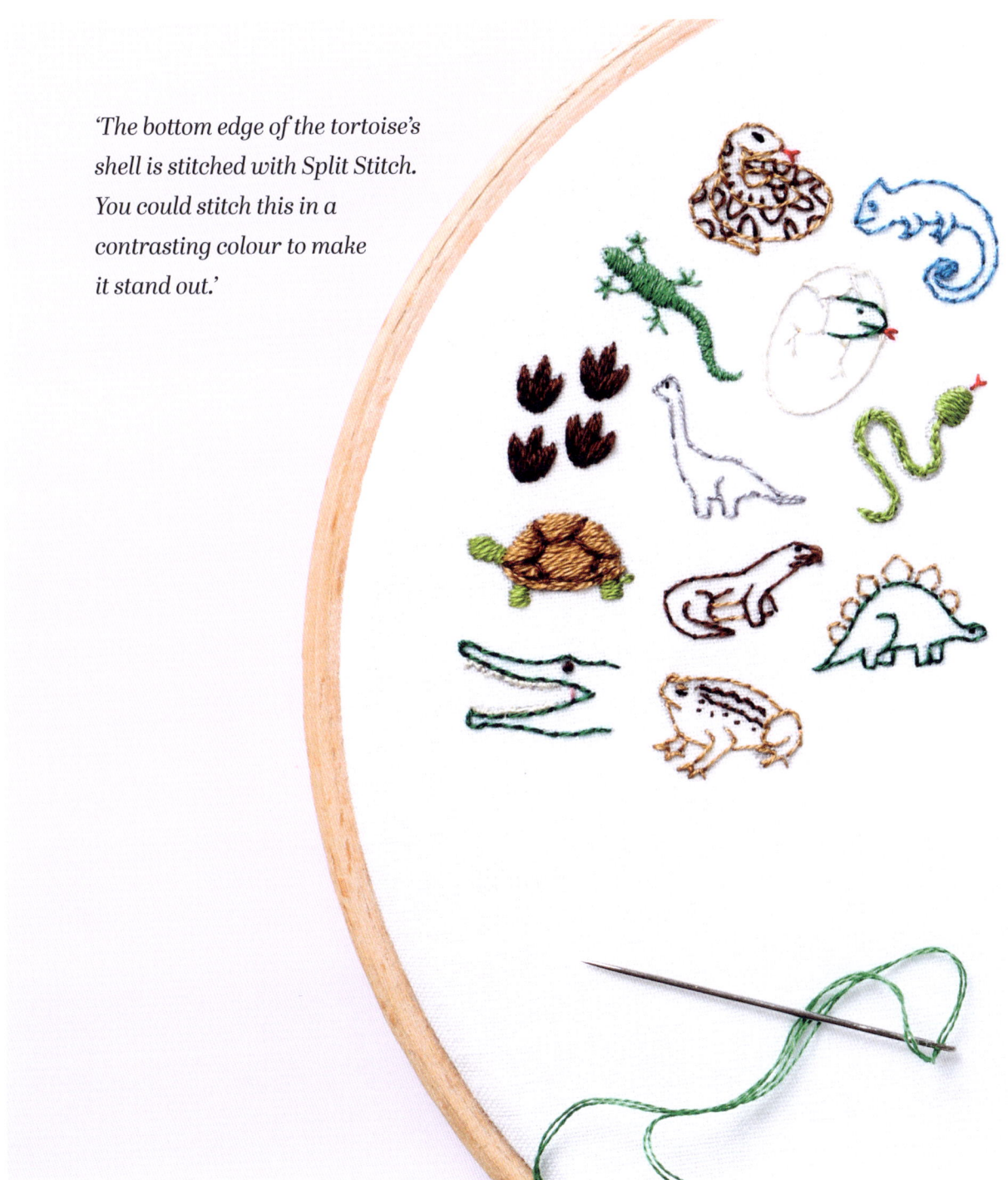

ANIMALS

Zoo Animals

COLOURS

Yellow 972
Peach 754
Orange 946
Red 321
Burgundy 814
Deep pink 600
Pink 603
Lilac 554
Purple 552
Deep blue 798
Blue 334
Pale blue 3841
Teal 3809
Green 701
Moss green 581
Dark green 3818
Brown 898
Tan 167
Beige 739
Grey 414
White BLANC
Black 310

Lion
Yellow, Orange, Tan, Black
French Knot, Satin Stitch, Scallop Stitch, Straight Stitch

Giraffe
Yellow, Tan, Black
Satin Stitch, Seed Stitch, Straight Stitch, French Knot

Elephant
Grey, Beige, Black
Back Stitch, Scallop Stitch, Seed Stitch

Gorilla
Grey, Black
Satin Stitch, Seed Stitch Scallop Stitch

Polar Bear
Beige, Black
Split Stitch, Scallop Stitch, Satin Stitch, Seed Stitch

Camel
Tan, Black
Satin Stitch, Straight Stitch

Kangaroo
Tan, Black
Back Stitch, Scallop Stitch, Seed Stitch

Koala
Tan, Grey, Beige
Straight Stitch, Back Stitch, Satin Stitch Seed Stitch

Tiger
Orange, Black
Scallop Stitch, Satin Stitch, Seed Stitch

Meerkat
Beige, Tan, Black
Seed Stitch, Scallop Stitch, Back Stitch

Rhino
Grey, Black
Back Stitch, Scallop Stitch, Seed Stitch

Panther
Black
Satin Stitch

Panda
Beige, Black
Satin Stitch

Monkey
Brown, Tan, Black
Scallop Stitch, Satin Stitch, Seed Stitch, Back Stitch

Lemur
Grey, Black, White
Scallop Stitch, Straight Stitch, French Knot, Back Stitch

Capybara
Tan, Black
Seed Stitch, Satin Stitch

Anteater
Grey, Beige, Black
Back Stitch, French Knot, Scallop Stitch

Zebra
Black, White
Straight Stitch, Scallop Stitch, Satin Stitch

Orangutan Face
Tan, Brown, Black
Satin Stitch, Scallop Stitch, Back Stitch, French Knot

Hippo Face
Brown, Beige, Pink, Black
Back Stitch, Scallop Stitch, Satin Stitch, French Knot

'The lion's mane is stitched using three colours to give it more depth. First, Satin Stitch the mane in orange floss, then go over it with a few straight stitches in yellow and tan.'

ANIMALS

Birds

COLOURS

Yellow 972
Peach 754
Orange 946
Red 321
Burgundy 814
Deep pink 600
Pink 603
Lilac 554
Purple 552
Deep blue 798
Blue 334
Pale blue 3841
Teal 3809
Green 701
Moss green 581
Dark green 3818
Brown 898
Tan 167
Beige 739
Grey 414
White BLANC
Black 310

Duck
Dark green, Tan, Beige, Orange, Yellow
Whipped Back Stitch, Straight Stitch, French Knot

Swallow
Beige, Grey
Satin Stitch

Swan
White, Black, Orange
Scallop Stitch, Back Stitch, Satin Stitch, French Knot

Flamingo
Pink, Deep pink, Black
Satin Stitch, Scallop Stitch, French Knot

Pigeon
Grey, Purple, Teal, Black
Back Stitch, Straight Stitch, French Knot

Toucan
Black, White, Orange, Teal
Satin Stitch, Scallop Stitch

Robin
Brown, Red
Back Stitch, Scallop Stitch, French Knot

Great Tit
Deep blue, Yellow, Black, Moss green, White
Back Stitch, Straight Stitch, Scallop Stitch, French Knot

Penguin
Black, White, Orange
Satin Stitch

Barn Owl
Tan, Beige, Black
Straight Stitch, Seed Stitch, Back Stitch, French Knot

Magpie
Black, White, Teal
Satin Stitch, Scallop Stitch

Ostrich
Pink, Black, Beige
Scallop Stitch, French Knot, Straight Stitch

Pelican
Pink, White, Tan
Scallop Stitch, Seed Stitch, Back Stitch, French Knot

Partridge
Orange, Tan, Black
Back Stitch, Scallop Stitch, French Knot

Eagle
Yellow, Beige, Brown
Scallop Stitch, Satin Stitch

Blue Jay
Deep blue, White, Black
Satin Stitch, Scallop Stitch, French Knot

Seagull
Grey, Yellow, Black, Beige
Whipped Back Stitch, Satin Stitch, French Knot

Hummingbird
Teal, Moss green, Purple
French Knot, Scallop Stitch, Back Stitch

Puffin
Black, White, Orange
Satin Stitch, Straight Stitch, French Knot

Kingfisher
Teal, Deep blue, Orange, Black
Back Stitch, Scallop Stitch, French Knot, Satin Stitch

'Scallop Stitch really comes into its own when outlining detailed motifs like these birds. You can easily change the size of the stitch by adjusting how long you make it and where you place the anchoring stitch.'

ANIMALS

Insects

COLOURS

Yellow 972
Peach 754
Orange 946
Red 321
Burgundy 814
Deep pink 600
Pink 603
Lilac 554
Purple 552
Deep blue 798
Blue 334
Pale blue 3841
Teal 3809
Green 701
Moss green 581
Dark green 3818
Brown 898
Tan 167
Beige 739
Grey 414
White BLANC
Black 310

Butterfly 1
Brown, Red, Yellow
Satin Stitch, Back Stitch

Butterfly 2
Deep blue, Brown
Satin Stitch, Back Stitch, Scallop Stitch, French Knot

Bee
Black, Yellow, Pale blue
Satin Stitch, Back Stitch, Straight Stitch

Worm
Pink
Back Stitch

Caterpillar
Moss green
Scallop Stitch, Back Stitch

Spider
Black
Satin Stitch, Back Stitch

Dragonfly
Purple, Teal
Straight Stitch, Satin Stitch, Scallop Stitch

Fly
Teal, Black, Pale blue
Satin Stitch, Back Stitch

Mosquito
Brown, Tan
Back Stitch, Straight Stitch, Satin Stitch

Wasp
Black, Yellow, Pale blue
Satin Stitch, Back Stitch, Straight Stitch

Shield Bug
Moss green, Brown
Satin Stitch, Back Stitch, Straight Stitch

Beetle
Black, Teal
Satin Stitch, Back Stitch

Ladybird
Red, Black
Back Stitch, Straight Stitch, Satin Stitch, French Knot

Snail
Brown, Tan
Back Stitch, Straight Stitch, Satin Stitch, French Knot

Slug
Grey, Tan
Back Stitch, Straight Stitch, Satin Stitch, French Knot

Moth
Brown, Tan, Grey
Back Stitch, Straight Stitch, Satin Stitch

Ant
Black
Satin Stitch, Back Stitch

Woodlouse
Brown, Tan
Scallop Stitch, Straight Stitch, Back Stitch

Grasshopper
Moss green
Scallop Stitch, Straight Stitch

Stick Insect
Brown
Back Stitch, Straight Stitch, Satin Stitch

'You can really have a lot of fun with these creepy-crawly motifs. Choose lifelike colours or use more playful ones to give the insects personality. You can also try adding tiny faces.'

ANIMALS

Pets

COLOURS

Yellow 972
Peach 754
Orange 946
Red 321
Burgundy 814
Deep pink 600
Pink 603
Lilac 554
Purple 552
Deep blue 798
Blue 334
Pale blue 3841
Teal 3809
Green 701
Moss green 581
Dark green 3818
Brown 898
Tan 167
Beige 739
Grey 414
White BLANC
Black 310

Pet Food
Brown, Grey, Tan
*Satin Stitch,
French Knot*

Goldfish Bowl
Orange, Yellow,
Tan, Pale blue
*Whipped Back Stitch,
Straight Stitch, Satin
Stitch, French Knot*

Bone
Beige
Satin Stitch

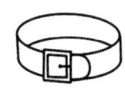
Collar
Red, Grey
*Straight Stitch,
Satin Stitch*

Kennel
Tan, Burgundy
Straight Stitch

Birdcage
Yellow, Grey
*Satin Stitch, Straight
Stitch, Scallop Stitch*

Hamster
Tan, Pale blue, Black
*Straight Stitch, Back
Stitch, Scallop Stitch,
French Knot, Satin Stitch*

Budgie
Yellow, Black, Moss green,
Beige, Deep blue, Tan
*Scallop Stitch, Back
Stitch, French Knot*

Dog
Beige, Black, Pink
*Scallop Stitch, French
Knot, Back Stitch*

Pet Carrier
Red, Grey
*Satin Stitch,
Back Stitch*

Dog Face
Black, Brown, Pink
*Back Stitch, Satin
Stitch, French Knot*

Paw Prints
Brown
*Satin Stitch,
French Knot*

Fish Skeleton
Pale blue
*Satin Stitch, Straight
Stitch, Scallop Stitch*

Leash
Tan, Grey
*Split Stitch, Scallop
Stitch, Satin Stitch*

Rabbit
Beige, Black,
Pink, Pale blue
*Straight Stitch, Back
Stitch, Scallop Stitch,
French Knot*

Cat Face
Black, Green,
Pink, Pale blue
*Scallop Stitch, Satin
Stitch, Back Stitch*

Cat
Black, Pink
Scallop Stitch

Sleeping Cat
Grey, Black
*Back Stitch, Scallop
Stitch, Satin Stitch*

Poodle
Beige, Black, Pink
*French Knot, Scallop
Stitch, Satin Stitch*

Labrador
Brown, Red
*Satin Stitch,
Scallop Stitch*

'You can easily tweak any of these pet designs to represent your furry friends. Swap stitches and colours to create your pet's special features.'

ANIMALS

Sea Life

COLOURS

Yellow 972
Peach 754
Orange 946
Red 321
Burgundy 814
Deep pink 600
Pink 603
Lilac 554
Purple 552
Deep blue 798
Blue 334
Pale blue 3841
Teal 3809
Green 701
Moss green 581
Dark green 3818
Brown 898
Tan 167
Beige 739
Grey 414
White BLANC
Black 310

Coral
Yellow
French Knot

Jellyfish
Peach, Lilac
Back Stitch, Straight Stitch, French Knot

Shark Fin
Grey, Teal
Satin Stitch, Scallop Stitch

Oyster
Peach, Beige, Tan
Satin Stitch, Split Stitch

Seahorse
Yellow, Orange, Black
Satin Stitch, French Knot

Plaice
Tan, Brown
Scallop Stitch, Seed Stitch, French Knot

Tropical Fish
Green, Pale blue, Black
Satin Stitch, French Knot

Fish
Grey, Blue
Satin Stitch, French Knot, Back Stitch

Clown Fish
Orange, Black, White
Satin Stitch, Scallop Stitch, French Knot

Blue Whale
Deep blue, Pale blue, Black
Satin Stitch, Split Stitch, French Knot

Octopus
Purple
Scallop Stitch, Lazy Daisy, Back Stitch

Crab
Orange, Brown
Satin Stitch, Straight Stitch, French Knot

Turtle
Brown, Tan, Moss green, Beige
Satin Stitch, Seed Stitch

Lobster
Red, Peach
Scallop Stitch, Back Stitch, Straight Stitch

Ray
Grey, Beige
Back Stitch, Scallop Stitch

Killer Whale
Black, White
Satin Stitch, French Knot

Squid
Peach, Black
Back Stitch, Scallop Stitch, French Knot

Shrimp
Orange, Black, Grey
Scallop Stitch, French Knot, Back Stitch

Dolphin
Pale blue, Black
Satin Stitch, French Knot

Seal
Grey, Black
Satin Stitch, French Knot

'Using Split Stitch on the underneath of the blue whale gives it a realistic look, mimicking the texture of the lighter part of its body.'

NATURE

Plants and Fungi

COLOURS

Yellow 972
Peach 754
Orange 946
Red 321
Burgundy 814
Deep pink 600
Pink 603
Lilac 554
Purple 552
Deep blue 798
Blue 334
Pale blue 3841
Teal 3809
Green 701
Moss green 581
Dark green 3818
Brown 898
Tan 167
Beige 739
Grey 414
White BLANC
Black 310

Bullrush
Tan, Brown, Green
Chain Stitch, Back Stitch

Falling Leaves
Red, Green, Orange, Brown
Back Stitch

Tree
Green, Moss green, Brown
French Knot, Back Stitch, Straight Stitch

Bare Tree
Brown
Straight Stitch

Fir Tree
Dark green, Brown
Split Stitch

Chestnut Leaves
Red, Brown
Back Stitch

Ash Leaves
Green
Back Stitch

Oak
Moss green
Back Stitch, Split Stitch

Simple Tree
Moss green, Brown
Satin Stitch

Three Mushrooms
Tan, Beige
Satin Stitch

Laurel
Green
Back Stitch, Scallop Stitch

Log
Brown
Back Stitch, Scallop Stitch

Shoot
Moss green, Brown, Green
Back Stitch

Beech Leaf
Orange, Brown
Back Stitch, Straight Stitch

Maple Leaf
Red, Orange
Scallop Stitch, Back Stitch

Toadstool
Red, White, Tan
Satin Stitch, French Knot

Mushroom
Brown, Beige
Back Stitch

Acorn
Brown, Tan
Back Stitch, Satin Stitch

Nest
Brown, Tan, Beige, Pale blue
Straight Stitch, Satin Stitch

Dandelion
Brown, White
Straight Stitch, Back Stitch, French Knot

'Depending on which month you stitch these designs, you could think about changing the colours so they are relevant to that season. For example, the tree stitched here in green would look great in shades of autumn.'

NATURE

Flowers

COLOURS

Yellow 972
Peach 754
Orange 946
Red 321
Burgundy 814
Deep pink 600
Pink 603
Lilac 554
Purple 552
Deep blue 798
Blue 334
Pale blue 3841
Teal 3809
Green 701
Moss green 581
Dark green 3818
Brown 898
Tan 167
Beige 739
Grey 414
White BLANC
Black 310

Pansy
Purple, Lilac
Satin Stitch, French Knot

Dandelion
White, Brown
Straight Stitch, Cross Stitch, French Knot

Rose
Red
Back Stitch

Daffodil
Orange, Yellow
Scallop Stitch, Straight Stitch, French Knot

Sunflower
Yellow, Brown, Tan
Scallop Stitch, French Knot

Water Lily
Pink
Scallop Stitch

Calla Lily
White, Yellow
Back Stitch, French Knot

Simple Flower
Pink, Yellow
French Knot, Straight Stitch, Scallop Stitch

Crocus
Purple, Yellow
Satin Stitch

Tulip
Red
Satin Stitch

Daisy
White, Yellow
Straight Stitch, French Knot

Hibiscus
Orange, Yellow
Scallop Stitch, Back Stitch, French Knot

Anthurium
Deep pink, Yellow
Back Stitch, Stem Stitch, French Knot

Fuchsia
Deep pink, Purple, Yellow
Scallop Stitch, Straight Stitch, French Knot

Forget-me-Not
Blue, Lilac, Yellow
Satin Stitch, French Knot

Dahlia
Burgundy
Scallop Stitch

Hydrangea
Blue
Scallop Stitch

Lavender
Lilac, Purple, Moss green
Lazy Daisy, Back Stitch

Blossom
Pink, Deep pink, Yellow
Satin Stitch, Straight Stitch, French Knot

Magnolia
White, Pink
French Knot

40

'Scallop Stitch is used quite a bit in this section as it's great for creating the curved lines of petals on the more intricate flowers with one strand of thread.'

NATURE

Weather

COLOURS

- Yellow 972
- Peach 754
- Orange 946
- Red 321
- Burgundy 814
- Deep pink 600
- Pink 603
- Lilac 554
- Purple 552
- Deep blue 798
- Blue 334
- Pale blue 3841
- Teal 3809
- Green 701
- Moss green 581
- Dark green 3818
- Brown 898
- Tan 167
- Beige 739
- Grey 414
- White BLANC
- Black 310

Sun
Yellow
Back Stitch, Straight Stitch

Rainbow
Grey, White
French Knot

Raindrops
Blue
Lazy Daisy

Lightning
Yellow
Satin Stitch

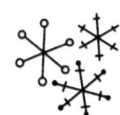

Snowflakes
Deep blue
Straight Stitch, French Knot

Thermometer
White, Red
Back Stitch, Straight Stitch, Satin Stitch

Sun Behind Cloud
Yellow, White
French Knot, Satin Stitch, Straight Stitch

Rain Cloud
White, Blue
Lazy Daisy, Back Stitch

Rain Cloud 2
Grey, Blue
Satin Stitch, Running Stitch

Rainbow with Clouds
Red, Yellow, Green, Blue, White
Back Stitch, Satin Stitch

Welly
Yellow, Brown, White
Satin Stitch

Wind
Teal
Back Stitch, French Knot

Wind Cloud
Grey, White
French Knot, Scallop Stitch

Lightning Cloud
Grey, Yellow
Back Stitch, Straight Stitch

Snow Cloud
Pale blue
Straight Stitch, French Knot

Two Clouds
Pale blue, White
French Knot

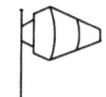

Wind Sock
Grey, Orange
Straight Stitch, Back Stitch

Sun and Cloud
Yellow, White
French Knot, Straight Stitch, Satin Stitch

Snowman
White, Brown, Black, Orange
Back Stitch, Straight Stitch, French Knot

Umbrella
Red, Grey, Tan
Back Stitch, Scallop Stitch, French Knot

42

'I always think clouds look fluffy when stitched using French knots. However, you could try other stitches such as Satin or Chain for a different texture.'

HOME

Houseplants

COLOURS

Yellow 972
Peach 754
Orange 946
Red 321
Burgundy 814
Deep pink 600
Pink 603
Lilac 554
Purple 552
Deep blue 798
Blue 334
Pale blue 3841
Teal 3809
Green 701
Moss green 581
Dark green 3818
Brown 898
Tan 167
Beige 739
Grey 414
White BLANC
Black 310

Desert Cactus
Dark green, Teal
Back Stitch, Straight Stitch, Scallop Stitch

Barrel Cactus
Green, Deep pink, Orange
Back Stitch, Lazy Daisy, Straight Stitch

Bunny Ear Cactus
Green, Tan
Straight Stitch, Back Stitch, Seed Stitch

Round Cactus
Moss green, Deep pink
Back Stitch, Straight Stitch, Scallop Stitch

Three Cacti Tray
Dark green, Moss green, Grey
Straight Stitch, Scallop Stitch

Daisies
Blue, Dark green, Yellow
Straight Stitch, Scallop Stitch

String of Pearls
Dark green, Green, Deep pink
French Knot, Back Stitch

Hanging Basket with Flowers
Pink, Purple, Tan
Back Stitch, Lazy Daisy

Cast Iron Plant
Green, Teal, Orange
Back Stitch, Straight Stitch, Scallop Stitch

Pilea
Moss green, Beige
Scallop Stitch, French Knot, Straight Stitch

Calathea
Green, Tan
Scallop Stitch, Back Stitch

Aloe Vera
Green, Deep pink
Back Stitch, Straight Stitch

Monstera
Dark green, Deep blue
Straight Stitch, Scallop Stitch

Monstera Leaf
Green
Scallop Stitch, Straight Stitch

Dahlia in Vase
Yellow, Green, Blue, White
French Knot, Scallop Stitch, Back Stitch

Vase with Foliage
Green, Pink
Lazy Daisy, Back Stitch

Flowers in Vase
Deep pink, Dark green, Yellow
Back Stitch, Scallop Stitch, Lazy Daisy, French Knot

Snake Plant
Green, Orange, Yellow
Back Stitch, Straight Stitch, French Knot

Rubber Plant
Moss green, Lilac
Satin Stitch, Scallop Stitch, Back Stitch

Trailing Plant in Hanging Basket
Dark green, White, Tan
Scallop Stitch, Straight Stitch

'You can play around with different stitches and shades of green to personalise these plant motifs. You could also stitch the plant pots in colours or designs similar to ones you have at home.'

HOME

Home Improvement

COLOURS

Yellow 972
Peach 754
Orange 946
Red 321
Burgundy 814
Deep pink 600
Pink 603
Lilac 554
Purple 552
Deep blue 798
Blue 334
Pale blue 3841
Teal 3809
Green 701
Moss green 581
Dark green 3818
Brown 898
Tan 167
Beige 739
Grey 414
White BLANC
Black 310

Ladder
Brown
Straight Stitch, Satin Stitch

Spanner
Grey
Satin Stitch

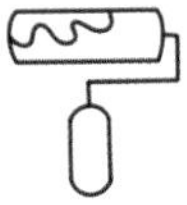

Paint Roller
Beige, Tan, Teal, Grey
Straight Stitch, Satin Stitch

Drill
Dark green, Black, Grey
Back Stitch, Straight Stitch, Scallop Stitch

Screwdriver
Orange, Grey
Straight Stitch, Back Stitch, Scallop Stitch

Trowel
Dark green, Grey
Back Stitch, Scallop Stitch

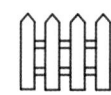

Picket Fence
Tan
Straight Stitch, Back Stitch

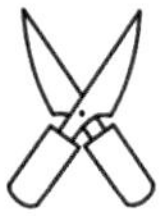

Shears
Grey, Tan
Back Stitch

Wheelbarrow
Dark green, Black, Grey
Satin Stitch, French Knot, Back Stitch

Compost
Brown, Tan, Black, Yellow
Satin Stitch, French Knot

Screw
Grey
Straight Stitch, Back Stitch

Saw
Red, Grey
Back Stitch

Hammer
Grey, Tan
Satin Stitch

Pliers
Grey, Red
Back Stitch, Scallop Stitch

Garden Fork
Dark green, Grey
Satin Stitch

Spade
Tan, Grey
Back Stitch, Scallop Stitch

Watering Can
Dark green
Back Stitch, Scallop Stitch

Boot
Red
Back Stitch

Lawn Mower
Dark green, Black
Straight Stitch, French Knot, Back Stitch

Tap
Grey
Split Stitch

46

'These motifs will have a totally different feel depending on which stitches you use; the boot or saw would look great satin-stitched to give them a more solid feel.'

HOME

Cooking

COLOURS

Yellow 972
Peach 754
Orange 946
Red 321
Burgundy 814
Deep pink 600
Pink 603
Lilac 554
Purple 552
Deep blue 798
Blue 334
Pale blue 3841
Teal 3809
Green 701
Moss green 581
Dark green 3818
Brown 898
Tan 167
Beige 739
Grey 414
White BLANC
Black 310

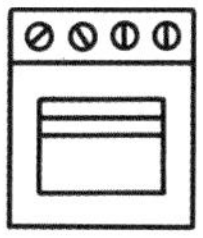

Oven
Grey, Black, Pale blue
Straight Stitch, Scallop Stitch

Apron
Beige, Black
Satin Stitch, Back Stitch, Scallop Stitch

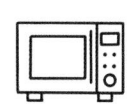

Microwave
Grey, Pale blue, Black
Straight Stitch, French Knot

Oven Glove
Grey
Straight Stitch, Back Stitch, Scallop Stitch, Lazy Daisy

Kettle
Yellow, Grey, Pale blue
Back Stitch, Scallop Stitch, Straight Stitch

Toaster
Tan, Grey, Red
Satin Stitch

Scales
Grey, Beige
Straight Stitch, Scallop Stitch, French Knot, Back Stitch

Chef's Hat
Beige
Scallop Stitch, Straight Stitch

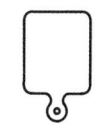

Chopping Board
Tan
Satin Stitch

Whisk
Grey
Stem Stitch, Satin Stitch

Mixer
Pink, Grey, Beige
Back Stitch, Straight Stitch, Scallop Stitch, French Knot

Piping Bag
Pink, Beige, Grey
Satin Stitch, Split Stitch

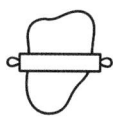

Rolling Pin
Tan, Beige
Satin Stitch

Jug
Pale blue, Grey
Straight Stitch, Split Stitch

Saucepan
Pale blue, Grey, Black
Satin Stitch, Straight Stitch, Scallop Stitch

Mixing Bowl
Beige, Tan
Straight Stitch, Scallop Stitch, Back Stitch

Knife
Grey, Black
Satin Stitch

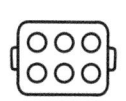

Muffin Tin
Grey
Satin Stitch

Pizza Oven
Orange, Grey, Burgundy
Satin Stitch, Back Stitch, Straight Stitch, Scallop Stitch

Pizza Cutter
Grey, Red
Satin Stitch, Scallop Stitch, French Knot

'Use these motifs when you've had a day of baking or batch cooking. You could also add a few Lazy Daisy "splats" if it ended up a bit messy!'

FOOD AND DRINK

Food

COLOURS

Yellow 972
Peach 754
Orange 946
Red 321
Burgundy 814
Deep pink 600
Pink 603
Lilac 554
Purple 552
Deep blue 798
Blue 334
Pale blue 3841
Teal 3809
Green 701
Moss green 581
Dark green 3818
Brown 898
Tan 167
Beige 739
Grey 414
White BLANC
Black 310

Pancakes
Beige, Tan, Yellow
Straight Stitch, Scallop Stitch, Back Stitch, Satin Stitch

Croissant
Tan, Brown
Satin Stitch, Straight Stitch

Pretzel
Tan
Stem Stitch

Bag of Crisps
Red, Yellow, White
Satin Stitch, Back Stitch, Straight Stitch

Cheese
Yellow
Straight Stitch, Scallop Stitch

Sausage
Brown
Back Stitch

Bacon
Burgundy, Beige
Split Stitch

Fried Egg
White, Yellow
Satin Stitch

Pasty
Tan
Back Stitch, Scallop Stitch

Loaf of Bread
Tan, Brown
Satin Stitch, Back Stitch

Slice of Bread
Beige, Tan
Split Stitch, Seed Stitch

Porridge
Red, Burgundy, Beige, Pale blue, Grey
Satin Stitch, French Knot, Scallop Stitch

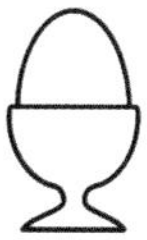

Boiled Egg
Blue, White, Peach
Satin Stitch, French Knot

Jam
Red, Yellow, Green, Pale blue
Satin Stitch, Back Stitch, Straight Stitch

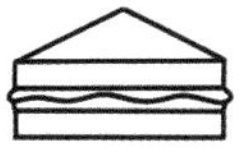

Sandwich
Beige, Green, Pink
Straight Stitch, Scallop Stitch

Bagel
Tan, Beige
Scallop Stitch, Back Stitch

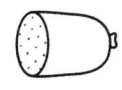

Salami
Burgundy, Pink
Seed Stitch, Back Stitch, Lazy Daisy

Bowl of Soup
White, Red, Pale blue
Satin Stitch, Back Stitch, Scallop Stitch

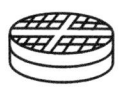

Waffle
Beige, Tan
Straight Stitch, Back Stitch

Baked Potato
Yellow, Orange, Tan
Satin Stitch, Scallop Stitch, Bullion Knot

'You can simplify or add more detail to any of these designs. If the baked potato with all the fillings looks a bit tricky, you could just stitch the outlines, or try making the pancake stack look a bit more three-dimensional by layering Satin Stitch.'

FOOD AND DRINK

More Food

COLOURS

Yellow 972
Peach 754
Orange 946
Red 321
Burgundy 814
Deep pink 600
Pink 603
Lilac 554
Purple 552
Deep blue 798
Blue 334
Pale blue 3841
Teal 3809
Green 701
Moss green 581
Dark green 3818
Brown 898
Tan 167
Beige 739
Grey 414
White BLANC
Black 310

Burger
Brown, Tan, Moss green, Red, Beige
Back Stitch, Seed Stitch, Scallop Stitch

French Fries
Yellow, Red
Satin Stitch, Straight Stitch, Bullion Knot

Hotdog
Tan, Brown, Red
Back Stitch, Scallop Stitch, Split Stitch

Pizza
Tan, Yellow, Pink, Burgundy
Straight Stitch, Satin Stitch, Scallop Stitch

Takeaway Noodles
Tan, Pale blue, Beige
Straight Stitch, Scallop Stitch, Lazy Daisy

Salad
White, Purple, Red, Green, Moss green
Scallop Stitch, Satin Stitch, Straight Stitch

Roast Chicken
Beige, Tan
Satin Stitch

Taco
Tan, Moss green, Red, Brown
Back Stitch, Scallop Stitch

Steak
Brown
Back Stitch, Straight Stitch

Kebab
Tan, Red, Beige, Green
Satin Stitch

Spaghetti
Pale blue, Beige, Grey
Split Stitch, Satin Stitch, Straight Stitch

Sushi
Dark green, White, Red, Moss green
Satin Stitch, Seed Stitch

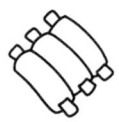

Ribs
Brown, Beige
Satin Stitch

Salmon
Pink, Grey
Scallop Stitch, Back Stitch, Straight Stitch

Farfalle Pasta
Tan
Straight Stitch, Scallop Stitch

Meatloaf
Brown, Tan, Burgundy
Back Stitch, Scallop Stitch, Seed Stitch

Meat Joint
Pink, Brown, Beige
Satin Stitch

Corn Dog
Tan, Yellow, Red
Back Stitch, Split Stitch, French Knot

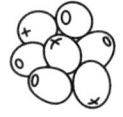

Olives
Moss green, Red
Scallop Stitch, Satin Stitch, Cross Stitch

Sausage Roll
Tan, Pink
Satin Stitch, Scallop Stitch, Back Stitch

'Bullion Knots make great French fries! Try stitching the ones in the background in Satin Stitch so they're not too bulky, then stitch those in the foreground with Bullion Knots to make them stand out.'

FOOD AND DRINK

Fruit and Veg

COLOURS

Yellow 972
Peach 754
Orange 946
Red 321
Burgundy 814
Deep pink 600
Pink 603
Lilac 554
Purple 552
Deep blue 798
Blue 334
Pale blue 3841
Teal 3809
Green 701
Moss green 581
Dark green 3818
Brown 898
Tan 167
Beige 739
Grey 414
White BLANC
Black 310

Lemon
Yellow
Stem Stitch, Seed Stitch

Pear
Moss green, Brown
Satin Stitch, Stem Stitch

Apple
Red, Brown, Moss green
Back Stitch, Straight Stitch, Lazy Daisy

Kiwi
Brown, Moss green, Beige, Black
Satin Stitch, Seed Stitch, Back Stitch

Strawberry
Red, Yellow, Green
Back Stitch, Seed Stitch, Scallop Stitch

Banana
Yellow, Brown
Split Stitch, Stem Stitch, Satin Stitch

Grapes
Burgundy, Brown, Green
Satin Stitch, Scallop Stitch

Watermelon
Deep pink, Dark green, Black
Straight Stitch, Split Stitch, Back Stitch, Seed Stitch

Orange
Orange, Beige
Back Stitch, Straight Stitch, Lazy Daisy Stitch, French Knot Stitch

Cherries
Burgundy, Green
Satin Stitch, Back Stitch

Avocado
Moss green, Dark green, Brown
Satin Stitch, Back Stitch

Broccoli
Green, Moss green
Satin Stitch, French Knot

Pepper
Red, Dark green
Satin Stitch

Carrot
Orange, Green, Brown
Satin Stitch, Lazy Daisy, Straight Stitch, Bullion Knot (Under the Satin Stitch)

Sweetcorn
Yellow, Tan Moss green
Satin Stitch, French Knot

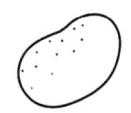

Potato
Beige, Tan
Back Stitch, Seed Stitch

Onion
Purple, Lilac, Peach
Back Stitch, Scallop Stitch, Seed Stitch

Aubergine
Purple, Moss green
Satin Stitch

Cabbage
Moss green, Beige
Satin Stitch

Chilli
Red, Green
Satin Stitch, Split Stitch

'The carrot is stitched using a Bullion Knot with Satin Stitch over the top to give it more structure. It's a really simple way to give more depth to your embroidery.'

FOOD AND DRINK

Drinks

COLOURS

Yellow 972
Peach 754
Orange 946
Red 321
Burgundy 814
Deep pink 600
Pink 603
Lilac 554
Purple 552
Deep blue 798
Blue 334
Pale blue 3841
Teal 3809
Green 701
Moss green 581
Dark green 3818
Brown 898
Tan 167
Beige 739
Grey 414
White BLANC
Black 310

Bottle of Pop
Brown, Red, Pale blue
Scallop Stitch, French Knot

Takeaway Drink
Red, White
Satin Stitch, Split Stitch

Glass of Pop
Pale blue, Orange
Straight Stitch, French Knot

Martini
White, Brown, Moss green
Straight Stitch, Satin Stitch

Beer
Tan, Beige, Pale blue
Satin Stitch, Back Stitch, French Knot, Straight Stitch

Red Wine
Burgundy, Pale blue
Satin Stitch, Back Stitch, Straight Stitch

Cocktail
Orange, Yellow, Pale blue, White
Satin Stitch, Back Stitch, French Knot

Spirit Glass
White, Pale blue, Tan
Straight Stitch, Back Stitch

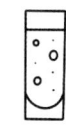

Wine Glass
Pale blue, Beige
Satin Stitch, Straight Stitch

Champagne Flute
Beige, Tan
Straight Stitch, Back Stitch

Tall Glass
Pale blue, Beige
Straight Stitch, Scallop Stitch, French Knot

Hot Drink
Deep blue, Pale blue
Back Stitch, Scallop Stitch

Hot Chocolate
Red, Beige
Satin Stitch, Split Stitch, Scallop Stitch

Tea
Tan, Beige, Pale blue
Scallop Stitch, Split Stitch, Straight Stitch

Latte
White, Beige, Tan
Stem Stitch, Whipped Back Stitch, Straight Stitch

Coffee Beans
Tan, Brown
Satin Stitch

Tea Bag
Beige, Tan, Brown
Straight Stitch, Split Stitch, French Knot

Coffee Pot
Brown, Black, Pale blue
Satin Stitch, Back Stitch, Straight Stitch

Teapot
Red, Burgundy
Satin Stitch, Scallop Stitch

Takeaway Coffee
White, Tan
Straight Stitch, Scallop Stitch

56

'The red wine glass could
be made into a gin glass
by stitching the liquid in a pale
colour. You could customise the hot drink
by stitching it in a different colour or adding
embellishments like spots or stripes!'

FOOD AND DRINK

Sweet Treats

COLOURS

Yellow 972
Peach 754
Orange 946
Red 321
Burgundy 814
Deep pink 600
Pink 603
Lilac 554
Purple 552
Deep blue 798
Blue 334
Pale blue 3841
Teal 3809
Green 701
Moss green 581
Dark green 3818
Brown 898
Tan 167
Beige 739
Grey 414
White BLANC
Black 310

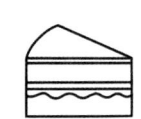

Cake Slice
Pink, Deep pink, Tan
Straight Stitch, Scallop Stitch, Back Stitch

Banana Split
Yellow, Beige, White, Red, Brown, Pale blue
Satin Stitch, Scallop Stitch, Straight Stitch

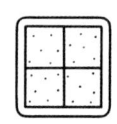

Battenburg
Pink, Yellow, Beige
Split Stitch, Satin Stitch

Meringue
Beige
Spit Stitch

Muffin
Beige, Brown, Tan
Satin Stitch

Profiteroles
Tan, Brown
Satin Stitch, Scallop Stitch

Ice Cream Sundae
Pale blue, Brown, Tan
Scallop Stitch, Straight Stitch

Cupcake with Cherry
Purple, Beige, Tan, Red
Satin Stitch, Straight Stitch

Cake on Stand
White, Red, Pink, Tan
Straight Stitch, Scallop Stitch, Seed Stitch

S'more
Tan, Beige, Brown
Straight Stitch, Scallop Stitch

Macaron
Deep pink, Pink
Back Stitch

Oreo
Brown, Beige
Running Stitch, Scallop Stitch, Back Stitch

Warm Pie
Beige, Grey, Pale blue
Straight Stitch, Scallop Stitch, Back Stitch

Slice of Pie (Egg Custard)
Yellow, Tan
Straight Stitch, Seed Stitch

Cookie
Tan, Brown
Satin Stitch

Cupcake
Beige, Tan
Straight Stitch, Satin Stitch

Doughnut
Tan, Pink, Blue, White
Split Stitch, Back Stitch

Iced Bun
Tan, White, Red
Satin Stitch, Scallop Stitch

Tart
Beige, Red
Satin Stitch, Scallop Stitch

Churros
Beige, White
Back Stitch, Seed Stitch

58

'You could really experiment with these motifs by making them more three-dimensional. Add seed beads for sprinkles or chocolate chips.'

FOOD AND DRINK

Sweets

COLOURS

Yellow 972
Peach 754
Orange 946
Red 321
Burgundy 814
Deep pink 600
Pink 603
Lilac 554
Purple 552
Deep blue 798
Blue 334
Pale blue 3841
Teal 3809
Green 701
Moss green 581
Dark green 3818
Brown 898
Tan 167
Beige 739
Grey 414
White BLANC
Black 310

Chocolate Bar
Purple, Yellow, Tan, Brown
Satin Stitch, Straight Stitch

Chocolate
Brown
Back Stitch

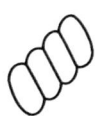

Marshmallow
Pink, Beige
Satin Stitch

Marshmallow 2
Beige
Satin Stitch

Gumball Machine
Red, Purple, Teal, Pale blue, Grey
Back Stitch, Straight Stitch, French Knot

Lollipop
Red, White
Stem Stitch, Straight Stitch

Lollipop 2
Pink, Beige
Back Stitch, Split Stitch

Wrapped Sweet
Deep blue, Blue
Satin Stitch, Straight Stitch

Wrapped Sweet 2
Teal, Orange
Satin Stitch

Boiled Sweet in Wrapper
Red, Pale blue
Satin Stitch, Straight Stitch, Scallop Stitch

Hershey's Kiss
Brown
Satin Stitch

Jelly Bean
Red, Peach
Satin Stitch, Scallop Stitch

Gummy Bear
Green
Scallop Stitch, Seed Stitch

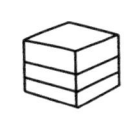

Liquorice Allsort
Black
Satin Stitch, Straight Stitch

Liquorice Allsort 2
Pink, Black
Satin Stitch, French Knot

Jelly Baby
Orange
Back Stitch, Scallop Stitch, Seed Stitch, French Knot

Cola Bottle
Beige, Tan
Satin Stitch, Straight Stitch

Cherries
Moss green, Red
Whipped Back Stitch

Love Heart
Deep pink, Beige
Satin Stitch

Banana
Yellow
Blanket Stitch, Back Stitch

'You can have loads of fun with these sweet designs. Try copying them smaller to show a pick and mix, or think about ways to make them really "pop" off the fabric!'

CELEBRATIONS

Wedding

COLOURS

Yellow 972
Peach 754
Orange 946
Red 321
Burgundy 814
Deep pink 600
Pink 603
Lilac 554
Purple 552
Deep blue 798
Blue 334
Pale blue 3841
Teal 3809
Green 701
Moss green 581
Dark green 3818
Brown 898
Tan 167
Beige 739
Grey 414
White BLANC
Black 310

Clinking Glasses
Pale blue, Tan
Straight Stitch, Scallop Stitch, Seed Stitch

Wedding Bells
Yellow
Back Stitch, Scallop Stitch, Straight Stitch

Top Hat
Grey, Pink
Satin Stitch

Bride
Pale blue, Peach, Yellow, Pink
Back Stitch, Scallop Stitch, French Knot

Groom
Brown, Grey, White, Peach
Satin Stitch, Straight Stitch, Scallop Stitch, French Knot

Engagement Ring
Yellow, Pale blue
Split Stitch, Straight Stitch

Wedding Dress
White, Pink
Scallop Stitch, Back Stitch, French Knot

Church
Grey, Tan, Pale blue
Straight Stitch, Scallop Stitch

Heart Sign
Tan, Beige
Straight Stitch, Scallop Stitch

Wedding Cake
Tan, Pink, Moss green, Grey, Deep pink
Scallop Stitch, Straight Stitch, Lazy Daisy

Bouquet
Pale blue, Deep pink, Yellow, Pink
Lazy Daisy, French Knot, Back Stitch, Scallop Stitch

Dove
Beige
Scallop Stitch, Back Stitch

Door Hanger
Beige, Red
Satin Stitch, Straight Stitch, Scallop Stitch

Wedding Invitation
Beige, Yellow, Grey, Pale blue
Straight Stitch, Scallop Stitch

Musical Hearts
Black, Deep pink
Satin Stitch, Straight Stitch

Save the Date
Red, Pale blue, Black
Straight Stitch, Seed Stitch, Satin Stitch, Scallop Stitch

Champagne
Dark green, Yellow, Red, Tan, Pale blue
Satin Stitch, Straight Stitch

Confetti
Pink, Lilac, Beige
French Knot, Satin Stitch

Wedding Ring
Grey, Yellow
Straight Stitch, Scallop Stitch, Split Stitch

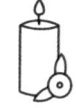

Candle
Beige, Yellow, Moss green, Deep pink
Scallop Stitch, Straight Stitch, French Knot

'Use these motifs to remember a wedding.
Try stitching the happy couple together, adapting
their skin and hair colours as appropriate.'

CELEBRATIONS

Easter

COLOURS

Yellow 972
Peach 754
Orange 946
Red 321
Burgundy 814
Deep pink 600
Pink 603
Lilac 554
Purple 552
Deep blue 798
Blue 334
Pale blue 3841
Teal 3809
Green 701
Moss green 581
Dark green 3818
Brown 898
Tan 167
Beige 739
Grey 414
White BLANC
Black 310

Egg with Butterfly
Green, Pale blue, Brown, Deep pink
Back Stitch, Straight Stitch

Chick
Yellow, Orange, Black
Back Stitch, French Knot, Straight Stitch

Hatching Chick
Yellow, Pale blue, Orange, Black
Back Stitch, French Knot, Straight Stitch

Easter Egg
Teal, Deep pink, Yellow
Back Stitch, French Knot

Easter Egg 2
Lilac, Pink, Blue
Back Stitch, Straight Stitch

Lamb
Grey, Black, White
French Knot, Satin Stitch, Back Stitch

Eggs
Blue, Lilac, Pink, Yellow
Satin Stitch

Easter Tree
Brown, Pink, Lilac, Yellow
Straight Stitch, Back Stitch, Scallop Stitch

Duckling
Yellow, Black, Orange
Back Stitch, French Knot, Straight Stitch

Egg Hunt Sign
Tan, Pink, Green
Straight Stitch, Scallop Stitch

Spring Flowers
Green, Pink, Lilac
Satin Stitch, Lazy Daisy, Back Stitch

Chick with Shell
Yellow, Pale blue, Orange, Black
Back Stitch, French Knot, Straight Stitch

Hot Cross Bun
Pink, Deep pink, Green
Lazy Daisy, Satin Stitch, Back Stitch, Scallop Stitch

Eggs in Basket
Tan, Pink, Pale blue
Split Stitch, Straight Stitch, Running Stitch

Birdhouse
Brown
Straight Stitch, French Knot, Scallop Stitch

Bunny
Grey, White, Black
Back Stitch, French Knot

Easter Wreath
Moss green, Pink, Lilac, Deep pink
Scallop Stitch, French Knot, Lazy Daisy

Egg with Bow
Pink, Deep pink
Back Stitch, Scallop Stitch

Jug of Flowers
Deep blue, Moss green, Deep pink
Back Stitch, Lazy Daisy

Easter Bunny
Grey, Pink, Black
Back Stitch, French Knot, Straight Stitch

'The big Easter eggs are super fun to stitch and would look great in a variety of shades. I always think pastels or paler shades work well for Easter to give a springtime feel.'

CELEBRATIONS

Birthday

COLOURS

Yellow 972
Peach 754
Orange 946
Red 321
Burgundy 814
Deep pink 600
Pink 603
Lilac 554
Purple 552
Deep blue 798
Blue 334
Pale blue 3841
Teal 3809
Green 701
Moss green 581
Dark green 3818
Brown 898
Tan 167
Beige 739
Grey 414
White BLANC
Black 310

Balloon
Red, Tan
*Back Stitch,
Scallop Stitch*

Gifts
Orange, Teal
*Straight Stitch,
Scallop Stitch*

Party Hat
Teal, Purple, Yellow
*Straight Stitch, Scallop
Stitch, Lazy Daisy*

Party Popper
Tan, Deep pink, Yellow
*Straight Stitch, Back
Stitch, French Knot*

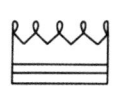

Crown
Yellow, Red
*Straight Stitch,
Lazy Daisy*

Star Balloon
Yellow, Tan
*Back Stitch,
Straight Stitch*

Bow
Deep pink
*Straight Stitch,
Back Stitch*

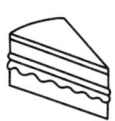

Slice of Cake
Tan, Pink, Red
*Straight Stitch,
Scallop Stitch*

Present
Yellow, Deep blue
Back Stitch

Balloon Dog
Yellow
*Scallop Stitch, Lazy Daisy,
French Knot*

Candle
Pink, Orange
*Lazy Daisy,
Straight Stitch*

Birthday Cake
Pink, Blue, Tan, Red
*Back Stitch, Scallop
Stitch, Straight Stitch,
Seed Stitch*

Birthday Card
Pale blue, Pink, Tan
Back Stitch, Lazy Daisy

Bunting
Teal, Orange
*Back Stitch,
Straight Stitch*

Bunch of Balloons
Pink, Purple, Teal, Yellow
*Back Stitch, Straight
Stitch, French Knot*

Long Balloon
Deep pink, Tan
*Satin Stitch, Lazy Daisy,
Back Stitch*

Streamers
Teal, Yellow, Deep pink
*French Knot, Back Stitch,
Lazy Daisy, Scallop Stitch*

Party Blower
Pink, Blue
*Straight Stitch,
Scallop Stitch*

Gift Bag
Yellow, Orange
*Straight Stitch,
Back Stitch*

Clown
Orange, Red, Black, Beige
*French Knot, Scallop
Stitch, Satin Stitch*

66

'These birthday motifs look great stitched in bright and cheerful shades. If you'd like to represent a more sophisticated party you've been to, they would also work well stitched in muted tones or in black and gold, for example.'

CELEBRATIONS

Valentine's Day

COLOURS

Yellow 972
Peach 754
Orange 946
Red 321
Burgundy 814
Deep pink 600
Pink 603
Lilac 554
Purple 552
Deep blue 798
Blue 334
Pale blue 3841
Teal 3809
Green 701
Moss green 581
Dark green 3818
Brown 898
Tan 167
Beige 739
Grey 414
White BLANC
Black 310

Heart
Red
Satin Stitch

Love Speech Bubble
Deep pink, Teal
Satin Stitch, Back Stitch

Love Letter
Pale blue, Black, Red
Split Stitch, Scallop Stitch, Satin Stitch

Lips
Red
Satin Stitch

Flower Bouquet
Pink, Deep pink, White
Lazy Daisy, Split Stitch, French Knot

Box of Chocolates
Brown, Purple
Satin Stitch, Scallop Stitch, Back Stitch

Bow and Arrow
Brown, Red
Back Stitch, Straight Stitch, Satin Stitch, Scallop Stitch

Heart and Arrow
Deep pink, Grey
Back Stitch, Straight Stitch

Three Hearts
Red, Pink, White
Back Stitch

Heart Balloon
Deep pink, Pale blue
Split Stitch, Lazy Daisy, Scallop Stitch

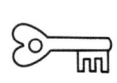

Key
Tan
Straight Stitch, Scallop Stitch

Lock
Grey, Black
Scallop Stitch, Back Stitch, Satin Stitch

Rose
Red, Dark green
Back Stitch, Scallop Stitch, Straight Stitch

Envelope
White, Red
Back Stitch, Scallop Stitch

Card
Red, Pink
Straight Stitch, Scallop Stitch

Heart Tag
Red, Pale blue, Tan
Satin Stitch, Straight Stitch, Scallop Stitch

Broken Heart
Red
Back Stitch

Love Potion
Teal, Deep pink, Pale blue
Satin Stitch, French Knot, Back Stitch

Flying Heart
Pink, Pale blue
Scallop Stitch, Back Stitch

Bear with Heart
Tan, Brown, Pink
Back Stitch, French Knot

'To make these motifs more personal you could try adding initials or a date; for example, this would work really well with the speech bubble, bear, letter or gift tag.'

CELEBRATIONS

Halloween

COLOURS

Yellow 972
Peach 754
Orange 946
Red 321
Burgundy 814
Deep pink 600
Pink 603
Lilac 554
Purple 552
Deep blue 798
Blue 334
Pale blue 3841
Teal 3809
Green 701
Moss green 581
Dark green 3818
Brown 898
Tan 167
Beige 739
Grey 414
White BLANC
Black 310

Ghost
White, Black
*Satin Stitch,
Back Stitch*

Pumpkin
Orange, Moss green, Black
Satin Stitch

Bat
Black, White
Satin Stitch, French Knot

Skull
Black
*Satin Stitch, Back Stitch,
Straight Stitch*

Spider Web
Black
*Straight Stitch,
Scallop Stitch*

Eerie Moon
Yellow, White
*Satin Stitch,
French Knot*

Black Cat
Black
Satin Stitch, Back Stitch

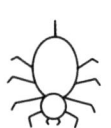

Spider
Black
*Satin Stitch,
Straight Stitch*

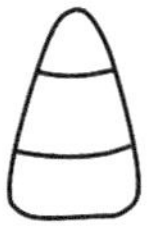

Candy Corn
Yellow, Orange, White
Satin Stitch

Fangs
White, Black
Satin Stitch, Back Stitch

Coffin
Brown
Straight Stitch

Zombie
Moss green, Red,
White, Black
*Back Stitch, Scallop
Stitch, Seed Stitch,*

Eyeball
White, Moss green,
Red, Black
Satin Stitch, Back Stitch

Witch's Hat
Purple, White, Yellow
*Back Stitch,
Straight Stitch*

Grave
Grey, Brown
*Back Stitch, Straight
Stitch, Scallop Stitch*

Sweets
Yellow, Orange, Purple
*Satin Stitch,
Straight Stitch*

Frankenstein's Monster
Moss green, Red,
Black, Grey
*Split Stitch, Straight
Stitch, French Knot*

Crossbones
White
*Straight Stitch,
Scallop Stitch*

Mummy
Black
Back Stitch, Satin Stitch

Spooky Eyes
Black
Back Stitch, French Knot

70

'If you'd like to stitch a larger motif, you could combine some of these designs; the skull and crossbones stitched using the same colour and stitches would look great!'

CELEBRATIONS

Christmas

COLOURS

Yellow 972
Peach 754
Orange 946
Red 321
Burgundy 814
Deep pink 600
Pink 603
Lilac 554
Purple 552
Deep blue 798
Blue 334
Pale blue 3841
Teal 3809
Green 701
Moss green 581
Dark green 3818
Brown 898
Tan 167
Beige 739
Grey 414
White BLANC
Black 310

Stocking
Red, Green, Beige
Satin Stitch, French Knot

Gift
Teal, Red
Satin Stitch, Back Stitch, French Knot

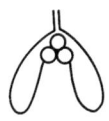

Bauble
Red, Yellow, Grey
Back Stitch, Satin Stitch, Lazy Daisy, Satin Stitch

Snowflake
Pale blue
Straight Stitch

Snow Globe
Blue, Green, Pale blue, Brown
Back Stitch, French Knot, Satin Stitch

Star
Yellow
Satin Stitch, Straight Stitch

Santa Hat
Red, White
Back Stitch, Satin Stitch

Candy Cane
Red
Back Stitch, Straight Stitch

Christmas Light
Pale blue, Grey
Satin Stitch

Bell
Yellow, Tan
Satin Stitch, French Knot, Lazy Daisy

Fir
Green
Straight Stitch, Back Stitch

Christmas Tree
Moss green, Yellow, Red, Brown
Back Stitch, French Knot

Decorated Tree
Moss green, Yellow, Brown, Red
Back Stitch, French Knot, Straight Stitch

Holly
Red, Green
Satin Stitch, Back Stitch

Angel
Yellow, Peach, Pale blue
Back Stitch, Satin Stitch

Cracker
Purple, Red, Blue
Satin Stitch, French Knot, Back Stitch

Wreath
Green, Moss green, Red
Seed Stitch, Satin Stitch, Back Stitch

Gingerbread Man
Tan, Brown
Split Stitch, French Knot

Rudolph
Red, Brown, Tan, Black
Satin Stitch, Back Stitch, French Knot

Mistletoe
Moss green, Beige
Back Stitch, French Knot

72

'These Christmas motifs can be stitched using a variety of stitches. The wreath looks great using two shades of green with layered seed stitches to give it that realistic feel, but you could swap these for Satin Stitch or French knots for a different texture.'

CELEBRATIONS

Religions and Celebrations

COLOURS

Yellow 972
Peach 754
Orange 946
Red 321
Burgundy 814
Deep pink 600
Pink 603
Lilac 554
Purple 552
Deep blue 798
Blue 334
Pale blue 3841
Teal 3809
Green 701
Moss green 581
Dark green 3818
Brown 898
Tan 167
Beige 739
Grey 414
White BLANC
Black 310

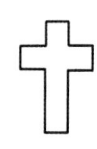

Crucifix
Tan
Satin Stitch

Rosary Beads
Grey, Brown
Back Stitch, French Knot

Ichthys symbol
Red
Satin Stitch

Shinto
Red, Yellow
Satin Stitch

Star of David
Deep blue
Straight Stitch

Menorah
Grey, Yellow
Split Stitch, Lazy Daisy

Hamsa Hand
Teal, Deep blue, Black
Back Stitch, Scallop Stitch, French Knot

The Crescent Moon and Star
Yellow
Satin Stitch, Straight Stitch

Prayer Mat
Deep blue, Yellow
Satin Stitch

Mosque
Yellow, Beige, Brown, Grey
Back Stitch, Straight Stitch, Scallop Stitch

Fireworks
Yellow, Pink, Teal
Satin Stitch, Seed Stitch, Back Stitch

Khanda
Deep blue
Satin Stitch, Back Stitch

Dharma Wheel
Yellow, Tan
Split Stitch, Scallop Stitch

Om
Red
Split Stitch, French Knot

Diyas (Diwali Candle)
Deep pink, Purple, Yellow
Back Stitch, Scallop Stitch, Straight Stitch

Four-leaf Clover
Moss green
Split Stitch, Straight Stitch, Scallop Stitch

Pilgrim Hat (Thanksgiving)
Black, Tan, Yellow
Satin Stitch, Straight Stitch

Chinese Lantern
Red, Yellow
Satin Stitch, Back Stitch, Straight Stitch

Poppy (Remembrance)
Red, Black, Dark green
Satin Stitch, French Knot

La Tomatina
Red, Dark green
Satin Stitch, Scallop Stitch, Stem Stitch

'You could customise the fireworks to match your celebration. For example, you could add the abbreviation of New Year's Eve (NYE) alongside the motif'.

WORK AND PLAY

Travel

COLOURS

Yellow 972
Peach 754
Orange 946
Red 321
Burgundy 814
Deep pink 600
Pink 603
Lilac 554
Purple 552
Deep blue 798
Blue 334
Pale blue 3841
Teal 3809
Green 701
Moss green 581
Dark green 3818
Brown 898
Tan 167
Beige 739
Grey 414
White BLANC
Black 310

Traditional Suitcase
Brown, Tan, White
Satin Stitch, Split Stitch

Backpack
Deep blue, Yellow, Blue
Satin Stitch, Scallop Stitch, Straight Stitch

Aeroplane
Pale blue, Yellow
Satin Stitch

Passport
Burgundy, Green, Blue
Straight Stitch, Satin Stitch

Map
Tan, Brown, Black
Straight Stitch, Scallop Stitch, Running Stitch, French Knot

Ship
Deep blue, Red, White, Black, Teal
Scallop Stitch, Straight Stitch, French Knot

Wheeled Suitcase
Grey, Black
Straight Stitch, Scallop Stitch

Train
Yellow, Pale blue, Grey
Satin Stitch, Straight Stitch

Yacht
White, Tan, Deep blue
Satin Stitch, Straight Stitch

Hot Air Balloon
Red, Orange, Yellow, Tan
Satin Stitch, Back Stitch, Straight Stitch

Globe
Moss green, Grey, Deep blue
Satin Stitch, Straight Stitch, Back Stitch

Aeroplane Window
Grey, White, Yellow
Split Stitch, Scallop Stitch, Satin Stitch, Straight Stitch

Camper Van
Orange, Beige, Grey, Blue, Black
Back Stitch, Scallop Stitch, Straight Stitch

Bicycle
Red, Black
Straight Stitch, Split Stitch

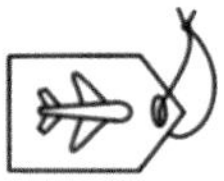

Luggage Tag
Tan, White, Grey
Back Stitch, Satin Stitch, Straight Stitch

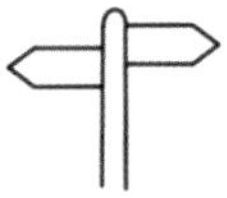

Direction Sign
Tan
Straight Stitch

Location Symbol
Red
Satin Stitch

Anchor
Deep blue
Straight Stitch, Scallop Stitch

Car
Red, Black, Yellow
Satin Stitch

Moped
Orange, Black, Grey
Scallop Stitch, Straight Stitch

76

'These travel motifs work really well to represent a holiday or trip you've been on and could be grouped together to show all of your adventures.'

WORK AND PLAY

Ball Sports

COLOURS

Yellow 972
Peach 754
Orange 946
Red 321
Burgundy 814
Deep pink 600
Pink 603
Lilac 554
Purple 552
Deep blue 798
Blue 334
Pale blue 3841
Teal 3809
Green 701
Moss green 581
Dark green 3818
Brown 898
Tan 167
Beige 739
Grey 414
White BLANC
Black 310

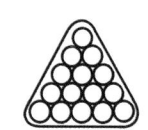

Snooker Balls
Red, Yellow, Black
Satin Stitch, Back Stitch

Baseball Bat and Ball
Grey, Black, Beige
Satin Stitch

American Football
Burgundy, Beige
Back Stitch, Satin Stitch, Straight Stitch

Golf Club and Ball
Grey, Beige
Straight Stitch, Seed Stitch, Back Stitch

Football
Black
Back Stitch, Satin Stitch, Straight Stitch

Ping Pong
Red, Tan, Pale blue
Satin Stitch

Volleyball
Black
Back Stitch

Bowling Ball and Pin
Beige, Red, Black
Back Stitch, Lazy Daisy, Satin Stitch

Softball
Beige, Red
Scallop Stitch, Whipped Back Stitch

Basketball
Orange, Black
Satin Stitch, Back Stitch

Tennis Ball
Moss green
Satin Stitch

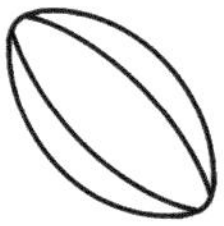

Rugby Ball
Brown, White
Satin Stitch, Straight Stitch

Tennis Racket
Teal, Pale blue, Black
Straight Stitch, Split Stitch, Satin Stitch

Cricket
Burgundy, Beige
Running Stitch, Back Stitch, Stem Stitch

Basketball Hoop
Tan, Red, Black
Straight Stitch, Scallop Stitch

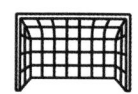

Football Goal
White
Split Stitch, Straight Stitch

Badminton Shuttlecock
Pale blue, Red
Straight Stitch, Scallop Stitch, Satin Stitch

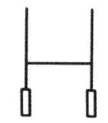

Rugby Posts
Beige, Deep blue
Straight Stitch, Satin Stitch

Hockey
Orange, Black
Scallop Stitch, Straight Stitch

American Football Helmet
Red, Grey, Black
Back Stitch, Scallop Stitch, French Knot

'Why not combine one of these motifs with a vest or pair of shorts from page 98? Change the colours of the clothes to represent your favourite team!'

WORK AND PLAY

Other Sports

COLOURS

Yellow 972
Peach 754
Orange 946
Red 321
Burgundy 814
Deep pink 600
Pink 603
Lilac 554
Purple 552
Deep blue 798
Blue 334
Pale blue 3841
Teal 3809
Green 701
Moss green 581
Dark green 3818
Brown 898
Tan 167
Beige 739
Grey 414
White BLANC
Black 310

Ice Skate
White, Black, Grey
Back Stitch, Straight Stitch, Scallop Stitch

Whistle
Grey
Satin Stitch, Straight Stitch, Scallop Stitch, Back Stitch

Boxing Glove
Red, Black
Back Stitch, Straight Stitch, Scallop Stitch

Rollerblade
Purple, Grey, Black
Straight Stitch, Scallop Stitch, French Knot, Seed Stitch

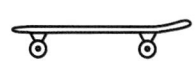

Skateboard
Black, Tan, Grey
Split Stitch, Scallop Stitch, Straight Stitch, French Knot

Running Shoe
Red, Beige, Grey
Straight Stitch, Scallop Stitch, Back Stitch

Archery Target
Red, Blue, Black, Yellow, Grey
Straight Stitch, Split Stitch

Trophy
Yellow, Black, Grey
Satin Stitch, Split Stitch

Medal
Grey, Red, Deep blue
Scallop Stitch, Straight Stitch

Ballet Shoes
Peach, Pink
Scallop Stitch, Back Stitch

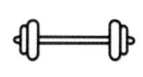

Weights
Grey, Black
Satin Stitch, Straight Stitch, Scallop Stitch

Rowing
Yellow, Deep blue, Black, White
Straight Stitch, Scallop Stitch, Back Stitch

Windsurfing
Red, Blue, White
Stem Stitch, Satin Stitch

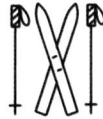

Skiing
Teal, Grey, Black
Straight Stitch, Scallop Stitch, Lazy Daisy

Surfboard
Orange, Tan
Satin Stitch, Split Stitch

Swimming
Deep blue
Satin Stitch, Scallop Stitch

Gymnastics
Tan, Blue, Brown
Scallop Stitch, French Knot

Fencing
Grey, Black
Straight Stitch, Satin Stitch, French Knot

Karate
White, Black
Straight Stitch, Scallop Stitch, Satin Stitch

Helmet
Orange, Black
Satin Stitch, French Knot, Split Stitch

'Tried out a new sport recently? Don't forget to customise the motifs to suit your experience!'

WORK AND PLAY

Hobbies

COLOURS

Yellow 972
Peach 754
Orange 946
Red 321
Burgundy 814
Deep pink 600
Pink 603
Lilac 554
Purple 552
Deep blue 798
Blue 334
Pale blue 3841
Teal 3809
Green 701
Moss green 581
Dark green 3818
Brown 898
Tan 167
Beige 739
Grey 414
White BLANC
Black 310

Yarn
Purple
Back Stitch, Straight Stitch, Split Stitch

Painting
Brown, Blue, Yellow, Tan
Straight Stitch, Satin Stitch, French Knot

Knitting Needles
Grey
Satin Stitch

Dominoes
Black
Straight Stitch French Knot

Cross Stitch
Tan, Deep pink, Grey
Cross Stitch, Split Stitch, Straight Stitch

Newspaper
Pale blue, Black
Straight Stitch

Crochet Hook
Grey, Deep pink
Satin Stitch

Museum
Grey
Straight Stitch

Needle
Grey, Pink
Straight Stitch, Back Stitch, Scallop Stitch

Pottery Wheel
Tan, Brown
Straight Stitch, Back Stitch

Paint Tube
Grey, Teal
Satin Stitch, French Knot

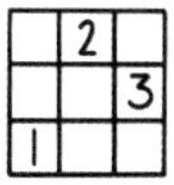

Sudoku
Black
Straight Stitch, Scallop Stitch

Paint Palette
Tan, Red, Yellow, Deep blue
Back Stitch, French Knot

Dart Board
Black, Red, Dark green
Straight Stitch, Back Stitch, French Knot

Pencil
Yellow, Tan, Grey, Pink
Straight Stitch, Scallop Stitch

Cooking
Grey, Tan
Satin Stitch, Scallop Stitch

Paintbrush
Tan, Grey, Teal
Satin Stitch, Scallop Stitch, Straight Stitch

Texting
Black
Straight Stitch, French Knot, Back Stitch

Easel
Tan, Beige
Straight Stitch, Scallop Stitch

Writing
Pale blue, Tan, Black
Straight Stitch, Scallop Stitch, Back Stitch

'Personalise these motifs by adding details such as a painting on the easel or change the cross stitch to a tiny embroidery or needle punch design.'

WORK AND PLAY

More Hobbies

COLOURS

Yellow 972
Peach 754
Orange 946
Red 321
Burgundy 814
Deep pink 600
Pink 603
Lilac 554
Purple 552
Deep blue 798
Blue 334
Pale blue 3841
Teal 3809
Green 701
Moss green 581
Dark green 3818
Brown 898
Tan 167
Beige 739
Grey 414
White BLANC
Black 310

Camera
Black
Back Stitch

Pin Cushion
Tan, Grey, Blue
Straight Stitch, French Knot, Back Stitch, Scallop Stitch

Binoculars
Grey
Straight Stitch, Scallop Stitch, French Knot

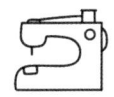

Sewing Machine
Pink, Teal, Grey
Back Stitch, French Knot, Straight Stitch

Open Book
Beige, Teal
Straight Stitch, Scallop Stitch

Bobbin
Tan, Deep pink
Straight Stitch, Scallop Stitch, Split Stitch

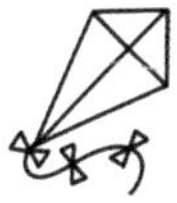

Kite
Red, Yellow, Blue
Straight Stitch, Back Stitch, French Knot

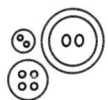

Buttons
Deep pink, Pink, Lilac
Back Stitch, French Knot, Scallop Stitch

Playing Cards
Black, Red
Back Stitch, Satin Stitch

Mannequin
Tan, Grey
Satin Stitch, Straight Stitch

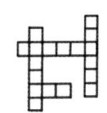

Crossword
Black
Straight Stitch

Origami
Teal
Straight Stitch

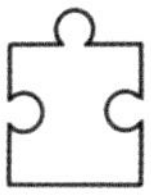

Jigsaw Piece
Orange
Straight Stitch, Scallop Stitch

Glue Gun
Black, Grey
Back Stitch, Scallop Stitch, Straight Stitch

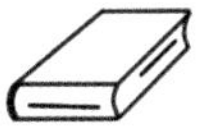

Book
Pale blue, Beige
Straight Stitch, Scallop Stitch

Scissors
Grey
Straight Stitch, Back Stitch, French Knot

Chess Piece
Beige
Straight Stitch

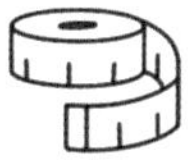

Tape Measure
Pink, Black
Back Stitch, Straight Stitch, Satin Stitch

Dice
Black
Straight Stitch, French Knot

Thimble
Grey
Back Stitch, French Knot

'Hobby motifs really lend themselves to adding more texture by incorporating other materials. You could use tiny seed beads for the heads of the pins in the pin cushion or make an appliqué jigsaw piece.'

WORK AND PLAY

Music

COLOURS

Yellow 972
Peach 754
Orange 946
Red 321
Burgundy 814
Deep pink 600
Pink 603
Lilac 554
Purple 552
Deep blue 798
Blue 334
Pale blue 3841
Teal 3809
Green 701
Moss green 581
Dark green 3818
Brown 898
Tan 167
Beige 739
Grey 414
White BLANC
Black 310

Electric Guitar
Red, Black, Tan
Straight Stitch, Scallop Stitch, French Knot

Treble Clef
Black
Scallop Stitch, Back Stitch, French Knot

Microphone
Black, Grey
Straight Stitch, Scallop Stitch, Split Stitch

Cassette Tape
Grey, Yellow
Straight Stitch, French Knot, Back Stitch, Scallop Stitch

Acoustic Guitar
Tan, Brown, Black
Straight Stitch, Back Stitch, Scallop Stitch

Piano
Black
Straight Stitch

Bongo
Tan, Purple, Deep pink
Straight Stitch, French Knot, Back Stitch

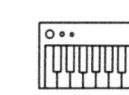

Keyboard
Black
Straight Stitch, Satin Stitch, French Knot

Flute
Grey
Straight Stitch, Scallop Stitch

Saxophone
Yellow, Tan
Straight Stitch, French Knot, Scallop Stitch

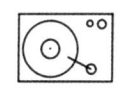

Record Player
Brown, Black, Grey
Straight Stitch, French Knot, Back Stitch

Maraca
Tan, Deep pink, Teal
Back Stitch, Scallop Stitch

Music Notes
Black
Satin Stitch, Back Stitch

Headphones
Black, Red, Grey
Satin Stitch, Back Stitch

Trumpet
Yellow
Straight Stitch, Back Stitch, Scallop Stitch

Drum
Grey, Red, Tan
Straight Stitch, French Knot

Speaker
Black, Deep pink
Straight Stitch, French Knot, Scallop Stitch

Xylophone
Tan, Brown, Grey
Straight Stitch, Running Stitch, French Knot

Radio
Teal, Grey
Straight Stitch, French Knot, Scallop Stitch

Violin
Tan, Brown, Black
Straight Stitch, French Knot, Back Stitch, Scallop Stitch

'Musical instruments are quite detailed by nature. If you're new to embroidery, you could always try simplifying them by taking out some of the smaller details. If you're a confident stitcher, try adding a person sat playing the piano or a face blowing the saxophone.'

WORK AND PLAY

The Great Outdoors

COLOURS

Yellow 972
Peach 754
Orange 946
Red 321
Burgundy 814
Deep pink 600
Pink 603
Lilac 554
Purple 552
Deep blue 798
Blue 334
Pale blue 3841
Teal 3809
Green 701
Moss green 581
Dark green 3818
Brown 898
Tan 167
Beige 739
Grey 414
White BLANC
Black 310

Compass
Tan, Red, Deep blue
Scallop Stitch, Back Stitch, Straight Stitch

Hiking Boot
Tan, Brown
Split Stitch, French Knot, Scallop Stitch

Flask
Teal, Grey
Back Stitch

Torch
Grey, Yellow
Satin Stitch, Straight Stitch

Sleeping Bag
Orange, Teal
Satin Stitch

Marshmallow
Tan, Beige, Brown
Back Stitch, Straight Stitch, French Knot

BBQ
Black, Grey
Satin Stitch, Straight Stitch, Scallop Stitch

Campfire
Red, Brown, Yellow
Satin Stitch, Bullion Knot

Binoculars
Black, Grey
Satin Stitch, Scallop Stitch

Canoe
Orange, Grey
Satin Stitch, Straight Stitch

Tent
Green
Straight Stitch

Carabiner
Red, Grey
Back Stitch, Scallop Stitch

Axe
Red, Grey
Satin Stitch

Paw Print
Brown
Satin Stitch, Back Stitch

Lamp
Grey, Yellow, White
Straight Stitch, Back Stitch, Satin Stitch

Map
Dark green, Black, Grey
Running Stitch, Cross Stitch, Back Stitch

Swiss Army Knife
Red, Grey
Straight Stitch, Scallop Stitch, French Knot

Mountains
Purple, White, Yellow
Split Stitch, French Knot

Forest
Dark green, Brown
Back Stitch

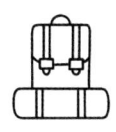

Backpack
Tan, Brown, Moss green
Back Stitch, Straight Stitch, Scallop Stitch

You can always adapt the motifs by changing a few specifics to reflect things you've experienced. This could be by altering the colour (is your tent red instead of green?), or by changing some of the smaller details, while using these designs for reference.'

WORK AND PLAY

At the Beach

COLOURS

Yellow 972
Peach 754
Orange 946
Red 321
Burgundy 814
Deep pink 600
Pink 603
Lilac 554
Purple 552
Deep blue 798
Blue 334
Pale blue 3841
Teal 3809
Green 701
Moss green 581
Dark green 3818
Brown 898
Tan 167
Beige 739
Grey 414
White BLANC
Black 310

Spade
Deep blue
Back Stitch

Sun
Yellow
Satin Stitch, Straight Stitch

Umbrella
Red, Brown, Tan
Back Stitch, Satin Stitch, French Knot

Coiled Shell
Peach
Satin Stitch

Snorkel
Black
Split Stitch

Bucket
Teal, Red
Satin Stitch, Back Stitch

Beach Ball
Red, White
Satin Stitch

Starfish
Orange, Yellow
Back Stitch, French Knot

Palm Tree
Moss green, Brown
Split Stitch, Blanket Stitch

Sunglasses
Pink, Black
Satin Stitch, Back Stitch

Flip-flops
Deep pink, Yellow
Back Stitch

Ice Cream
Tan, Brown, Pink, Beige
Straight Stitch, French Knot

Wave
Blue, Teal
French Knot, Back Stitch, Running Stitch

Birds
Red, Brown, Tan
Back Stitch, Satin Stitch, French Knot

Beach Mat
White, Blue
Back Stitch, Straight Stitch

Cockle Shell
Pale blue
Split Stitch

Shell
Beige
Back Stitch

Sandcastle
Tan, Brown, Red
Satin Stitch, Straight Stitch

Ice Lolly
Brown, Pink, Tan
Satin Stitch

Beach Hut
Blue, Red
Satin Stitch, Straight Stitch, French Knot

'Use a bright and sunny thread palette to stitch these beach-themed motifs. Experiment with different stitch types to create varying textures, such as swapping French knots in the ice cream for Satin Stitch.'

WORK AND PLAY

Entertainment

COLOURS

Yellow 972
Peach 754
Orange 946
Red 321
Burgundy 814
Deep pink 600
Pink 603
Lilac 554
Purple 552
Deep blue 798
Blue 334
Pale blue 3841
Teal 3809
Green 701
Moss green 581
Dark green 3818
Brown 898
Tan 167
Beige 739
Grey 414
White BLANC
Black 310

Clapper Board
Black
Straight Stitch

TV
Grey, Black
Straight Stitch, Scallop Stitch, French Knot

Theatre Stage
Black, Red
Straight Stitch, Scallop Stitch, French Knot

Movie Camera
Black
Straight Stitch, Back Stitch, French Knot

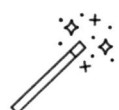

Magic Wand
Black, White, Yellow
Straight Stitch, Cross Stitch, French Knot

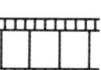

Film
Black
Straight Stitch

Magician's Hat
Black, Pink, Yellow
Satin Stitch, French Knot, Straight Stitch, Scallop Stitch

Circus Tent
Deep blue, Red
Satin Stitch, Scallop Stitch, Straight Stitch

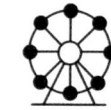

Ferris Wheel
Red, Deep blue, Grey
French Knot, Straight Stitch, Satin Stitch

Cannon
Grey, Red, Brown
Back Stitch, Satin Stitch, Straight Stitch

Cinema Ticket
Grey, Yellow, Red
Straight Stitch, Running Stitch, Scallop Stitch

Theatre Masks
Blue, Yellow
Scallop Stitch, Back Stitch

Oscar
Yellow, Black
Straight Stitch, Scallop Stitch

3D Glasses
Red, Blue, Grey
Straight Stitch

Popcorn and Drink
Red, Yellow, Deep blue
Straight Stitch, Scallop Stitch, Satin Stitch, Back Stitch

Gaming Controller
Black, Red, Grey
Satin Stitch, Back Stitch, French Knot

Carousel
Dark green, Red, Tan
Straight Stitch, Scallop Stitch

Slot Machine
Grey, Deep blue, Red
Straight Stitch, French Knot, Back Stitch

Concert
Grey, Purple, Black, Yellow
Straight Stitch, French Knot, Back Stitch, Scallop Stitch, Seed Stitch

Disco Ball
Grey, Yellow
Scallop Stitch, Straight Stitch

'You could personalise the theatre stage or TV motif by adding a symbol or characters to represent a show you have seen recently.'

WORK AND PLAY

Work and Education

COLOURS

Yellow 972
Peach 754
Orange 946
Red 321
Burgundy 814
Deep pink 600
Pink 603
Lilac 554
Purple 552
Deep blue 798
Blue 334
Pale blue 3841
Teal 3809
Green 701
Moss green 581
Dark green 3818
Brown 898
Tan 167
Beige 739
Grey 414
White BLANC
Black 310

Flash Drive
Red, Grey
Satin Stitch, Straight Stitch

Computer Monitor
White, Grey, Black
Straight Stitch, French Knot, Scallop Stitch

Mouse
Black
Back Stitch, Straight Stitch

Headset
Black, Grey
Back Stitch, Satin Stitch

Laptop
Black, Deep blue
Straight Stitch

Clock
Yellow, Grey, Black
Split Stitch, Straight Stitch, French Knot

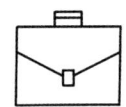

Briefcase
Tan, Grey
Satin Stitch, Straight Stitch

Printer
Grey, Pale blue, Yellow
Straight Stitch, Satin Stitch, French Knot

Clipboard
Tan, Grey, Pale blue, Black
Straight Stitch, Scallop Stitch

Scroll / Certificate
Pale blue, Red, Yellow
Straight Stitch, Back Stitch, Scallop Stitch

Graduation Cap
Black, Grey, Yellow
Satin Stitch, Straight Stitch

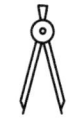

Compass
Grey, Red
Straight Stitch, Scallop Stitch, French Knot

Email
Red, Pale blue
Straight Stitch, Lazy Daisy, Back Stitch

Calculator
Orange, Deep blue, Grey
Straight Stitch

Notepad
Pale blue, Grey, Deep blue
Straight Stitch

Paperclip
Grey
Back Stitch

Ruler
Yellow, Black
Straight Stitch

Pen
Burgundy, Grey
Straight Stitch, Scallop Stitch

Phone
Beige, Grey
Straight Stitch, Scallop Stitch, French Knot

Lamp
Deep blue, Yellow, Grey
Satin Stitch, Split Stitch, Straight Stitch

94

'You could try incorporating wire into the graduation cap to make it stand up off the fabric.'

PERSONAL CARE

Beauty

COLOURS

Yellow 972
Peach 754
Orange 946
Red 321
Burgundy 814
Deep pink 600
Pink 603
Lilac 554
Purple 552
Deep blue 798
Blue 334
Pale blue 3841
Teal 3809
Green 701
Moss green 581
Dark green 3818
Brown 898
Tan 167
Beige 739
Grey 414
White BLANC
Black 310

Perfume
Teal, Grey, Black, Pale blue
Satin Stitch, Straight Stitch

Comb
Black
Satin Stitch

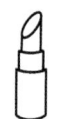

Lipstick
Red, Grey, Black
Straight Stitch, Scallop Stitch

Compact
Black, Pale blue, Peach
Scallop Stitch, Straight Stitch, Satin Stitch

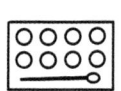

Eyeshadow
Black, Beige, Tan, Grey
Satin Stitch, Straight Stitch

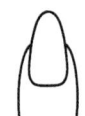

Nail
Deep pink, Peach
Satin Stitch, Split Stitch

Nail Polish
Red, Black, Grey
Satin Stitch, Straight Stitch

Hair Scissors
Grey
Straight Stitch, Scallop Stitch, French Knot

Eyebrow
Brown
Satin Stitch

Face Cream
Black, Beige
Satin Stitch

Mirror
Tan, Pale blue
Straight Stitch, Split Stitch

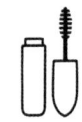

Mascara
Deep pink, Black, Grey
Satin Stitch, Straight Stitch

Make-up Brush
Black, Tan, Grey
Satin Stitch, Straight Stitch, Back Stitch

Tube of Cream
Beige
Back Stitch, Straight Stitch, Scallop Stitch

Blow Dryer
Black, Grey
Back Stitch, Scallop Stitch

Eyelashes
Blue, White, Black
Satin Stitch, Straight Stitch

Round Brush
Tan, Black
Straight Stitch, Satin Stitch

Hair Straighteners
Purple, Grey
Straight Stitch, Scallop Stitch

Clippers
Grey, Black
Straight Stitch, Scallop Stitch, Back Stitch

Curling Wand
Grey, Black
Straight Stitch, Scallop Stitch, Back Stitch

'Having a pamper night or getting dressed up for a special occasion? Try using one of these motifs to remember it by!'

PERSONAL CARE

Clothes

COLOURS

Yellow 972
Peach 754
Orange 946
Red 321
Burgundy 814
Deep pink 600
Pink 603
Lilac 554
Purple 552
Deep blue 798
Blue 334
Pale blue 3841
Teal 3809
Green 701
Moss green 581
Dark green 3818
Brown 898
Tan 167
Beige 739
Grey 414
White BLANC
Black 310

T-shirt
Beige
Satin Stitch

Vest
White
Straight Stitch, Scallop Stitch

Sweater
Orange, Beige
Chain Stitch, Straight Stitch

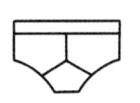

Briefs
White, Pale blue
Satin Stitch, Straight Stitch

Socks
Green
Scallop Stitch, Straight Stitch

Shirt
Pale blue, Blue
Back Stitch, Straight Stitch, French Knot

Trousers
Blue, Deep blue
Satin Stitch, Straight Stitch

Shorts
Yellow, Orange
Satin Stitch, Lazy Daisy, Straight Stitch

Hoodie
Deep blue
Back Stitch, Lazy Daisy

Cardigan
Beige, Tan
Split Stitch, Straight Stitch, French Knot

Skirt
Purple
Stem Stitch, Satin Stitch

Blazer
Burgundy, Black
Straight Stitch, Scallop Stitch, French Knot

Coat
Tan, Brown
Scallop Stitch, Straight Stitch, French Knot

Dress
Pink, Deep pink
Satin Stitch, Straight Stitch

Evening Dress
Black, Deep pink
Satin Stitch, Scallop Stitch

Bra
Red, Black
Satin Stitch, Straight Stitch

Polo Shirt
Blue
Scallop Stitch, Back Stitch, Straight Stitch

Blouse
Lilac
Back Stitch, Scallop Stitch

Leggings
Black
Satin Stitch

Gilet
Teal
Straight Stitch, Scallop Stitch

'The sweater is stitched using rows of Chain Stitch to give it some texture. You could try this on other knitted items such as the socks and cardigan or the bobble hat and mittens on the following page. If you're feeling adventurous, you could even give them some stripes!'

PERSONAL CARE

Shoes and Accessories

COLOURS

Yellow 972
Peach 754
Orange 946
Red 321
Burgundy 814
Deep pink 600
Pink 603
Lilac 554
Purple 552
Deep blue 798
Blue 334
Pale blue 3841
Teal 3809
Green 701
Moss green 581
Dark green 3818
Brown 898
Tan 167
Beige 739
Grey 414
White BLANC
Black 310

Analogue Watch
Brown, Grey, Black
Straight Stitch, Back Stitch, Satin Stitch

Digital Watch
Black, Grey
Straight Stitch, Back Stitch, French Knot

Sneaker
Grey, Red
Satin Stitch, Lazy Daisy, Back Stitch, Straight Stitch

Bobble Hat
Teal, Orange
Chain Stitch, French Knot, Back Stitch

Tie
Red, Blue
Satin Stitch

Belt
Brown, Yellow, Black
Back Stitch, Straight Stitch, French Knot

Baseball Cap
Deep blue, Red
Scallop Stitch, Straight Stitch

Smart Shoe
Black, Brown
Satin Stitch, Straight Stitch

Mittens
Green
Satin Stitch, Straight Stitch

Bow
Deep pink
Straight Stitch, Split Stitch

Scarf
Deep blue, White
Split Stitch, Straight Stitch

Boot
Brown, Black
Satin Stitch, Straight Stitch

Pearl Necklace
Peach, Grey
Satin Stitch, Lazy Daisy, French Knot

Bucket Hat
Blue
Satin Stitch

High-heeled Shoe
Red, Grey
Satin Stitch, Straight Stitch

Handbag
Tan, Brown, Grey
Split Stitch, Back Stitch, Satin Stitch

Glasses
Black
Back Stitch

Earrings
Purple, Yellow, Grey
Back Stitch, Satin Stitch

Sun Hat
Tan, Pink
Satin Stitch, Chain Stitch

Duffel Bag
Tan, Brown
Satin Stitch, Scallop Stitch, Straight Stitch

'The scarf is stitched using rows of Split Stitch, alternating between deep blue and white to give it a knitted texture. It's easier to start with the outlines and work your way in to make sure you keep the shape.'

CHILDREN

Baby

COLOURS

Yellow 972
Peach 754
Orange 946
Red 321
Burgundy 814
Deep pink 600
Pink 603
Lilac 554
Purple 552
Deep blue 798
Blue 334
Pale blue 3841
Teal 3809
Green 701
Moss green 581
Dark green 3818
Brown 898
Tan 167
Beige 739
Grey 414
White BLANC
Black 310

Dummy
Yellow, Beige, Grey
Satin Stitch, Split Stitch

Bottle
Pale blue, Beige, Pink
Scallop Stitch, Straight Stitch

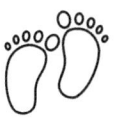

Footprints
Blue
Satin Stitch

Mobile
Tan, Pink, Yellow, Pale blue
Straight Stitch, Split Stitch, Satin Stitch, French Knot, Scallop Stitch

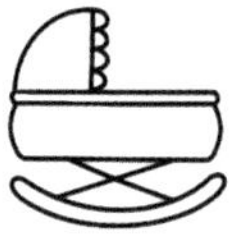

Moses Basket
Pink, Beige, Tan, Grey
Straight Stitch, Scallop Stitch, Back Stitch, Whipped Back Stitch

Safety Pin
Grey, Pale blue
Satin Stitch, Whipped Back Stitch

Bear Rattle
Black, Tan, Beige
Back Stitch, Scallop Stitch, French Knot

Rattle
Pink
Back Stitch, Scallop Stitch, Straight Stitch

Bear
Tan, Beige, Black
Scallop Stitch, Back Stitch

Sippy Cup
Yellow, Orange
Split Stitch, Satin Stitch

Pushchair
Orange, Grey, Black
Straight Stitch, Back Stitch, Scallop Stitch, French Knot

Pram
Blue, Grey, Black
Satin Stitch, Straight Stitch, Scallop Stitch, French Knot

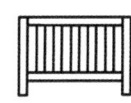

Crib
Tan
Straight Stitch

Nappy
Beige
Back Stitch, Satin Stitch

Baby Bath
Pale blue, Beige
Satin Stitch, Split Stitch, French Knot

Bib
Pale blue
Back Stitch, French Knot

Babygrow
White
Satin Stitch

Fork and Spoon
Blue
Scallop Stitch, Straight Stitch

Baby Face with Bow
Peach, Lilac, Black
Satin Stitch, Scallop Stitch, Whipped Back Stitch, French Knot

Baby Face with Dummy
Peach, Yellow, Black
Scallop Stitch, Stem Stitch, French Knot

'These cute baby motifs are totally adaptable. Think about which stitches you prefer to use. You don't have to stick with the suggested ones – the main thing is that you enjoy stitching your hoop!'

CHILDREN

Toys

COLOURS

- Yellow 972
- Peach 754
- Orange 946
- Red 321
- Burgundy 814
- Deep pink 600
- Pink 603
- Lilac 554
- Purple 552
- Deep blue 798
- Blue 334
- Pale blue 3841
- Teal 3809
- Green 701
- Moss green 581
- Dark green 3818
- Brown 898
- Tan 167
- Beige 739
- Grey 414
- White BLANC
- Black 310

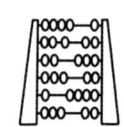

Abacus
Tan, Deep blue, Yellow, Grey
Satin Stitch, Straight Stitch, French Knot

Pull-along dog
Tan, Brown, Red, Grey
Satin Stitch, French Knot, Scallop Stitch

Water Pistol
Moss green, Orange, Deep blue, Blue
Satin Stitch, Lazy Daisy, Back Stitch

Skipping Rope
Tan, Deep pink
Satin Stitch, Scallop Stitch, Back Stitch

Wooden Train
Red, Blue, Yellow, Green, Black
Satin Stitch

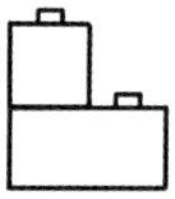

Interlocking bricks
Deep blue, Yellow
Satin Stitch

Ring Stacker
Brown, Tan, Beige
Satin Stitch

Dino
Green, Teal, Black
Back Stitch, Scallop Stitch, French Knot

Playdough
Yellow, Red, Blue
Satin Stitch, Scallop Stitch

Shape Sorter
Tan, Red, Yellow, Green, Blue
Straight Stitch, Satin Stitch

Yo-yo
Orange, Tan
Satin Stitch, Split Stitch

Wind-up Car
Red, Black, Yellow
Satin Stitch, Split Stitch, Scallop Stitch, French Knot

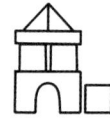

Building Blocks
Red, Blue, Yellow, Tan
Satin Stitch

Pinwheel
Teal, Orange, Tan
Straight Stitch

Fidget Spinner
Red, Black
Split Stitch

Rocking Horse
Tan, Brown, Beige
Straight Stitch, Scallop Stitch, French Knot

Dolly
Pink, Tan, Brown
Satin Stitch, Scallop Stitch, French Knot

Scooter
Grey, Black, Orange
Straight Stitch, Scallop Stitch, French Knot

Robot
Grey, Black, Red
Straight Stitch, French Knot

Spinning Top
Orange, Yellow, Deep blue
Straight Stitch, Scallop Stitch, French Knot

'You could customise any of these designs to represent a gift you have bought or a toy you treasure from your childhood.'

MIND, BODY, AND SPIRIT

Spiritual

COLOURS

Yellow 972
Peach 754
Orange 946
Red 321
Burgundy 814
Deep pink 600
Pink 603
Lilac 554
Purple 552
Deep blue 798
Blue 334
Pale blue 3841
Teal 3809
Green 701
Moss green 581
Dark green 3818
Brown 898
Tan 167
Beige 739
Grey 414
White BLANC
Black 310

Three Crystals
Pale blue, Grey
Straight Stitch, Scallop Stitch

Natural Crystal
Lilac
Straight Stitch

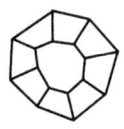

Ruby
Red
Satin Stitch

Crystal Wand
Beige
Straight Stitch

Smudging Stick
Brown, Tan
Straight Stitch, Lazy Daisy

Palm Reading
Peach, Black
Back Stitch, Running Stitch, Straight Stitch

Lotus
Deep pink, Pink, Teal
Back Stitch, Scallop Stitch

Om Hand
Peach
Scallop Stitch

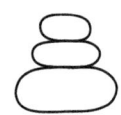

Rock Balancing
Grey, Pale blue, Beige
Satin Stitch

Yin Yang
Deep blue
Whipped Back Stitch

All-Seeing Eye
Black
Straight Stitch, Scallop Stitch, French Knot

Mandala 1
Blue, Deep blue, Teal
Back Stitch, Scallop Stitch, French Knot

Mandala 2
Red, Orange, Yellow, Moss green, Deep blue, Purple
Back Stitch, Scallop Stitch, Straight Stitch

Tree of Life
Brown
Back Stitch

Tarot Cards
Purple, Tan
Straight Stitch, Satin Stitch

Evil Eye
Blue, Deep blue, Black
Split Stitch, French Knot

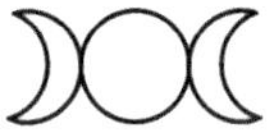

Triple Goddess
Purple
Back Stitch

Candle
Beige, Tan, Orange
Satin Stitch, Lazy Daisy, Back Stitch

Yoga Mat
Purple
Straight Stitch, Scallop Stitch

Seven Chakras
Grey, Yellow
Back Stitch, French Knot

'Adding the thin line of tan stitching under the dripping wax really gives the candle a more realistic look as it gives it more depth.'

MIND, BODY, AND SPIRIT

Astrology

COLOURS

Yellow 972
Peach 754
Orange 946
Red 321
Burgundy 814
Deep pink 600
Pink 603
Lilac 554
Purple 552
Deep blue 798
Blue 334
Pale blue 3841
Teal 3809
Green 701
Moss green 581
Dark green 3818
Brown 898
Tan 167
Beige 739
Grey 414
White BLANC
Black 310

Aries
Black
Back Stitch

Taurus
Purple
Split Stitch

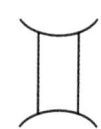

Gemini
Beige
Whipped Back Stitch

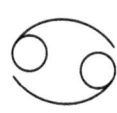

Cancer
Deep pink
Back Stitch

Leo
Teal
Split Stitch

Virgo
Deep blue
*Straight Stitch,
Scallop Stitch*

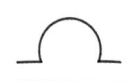

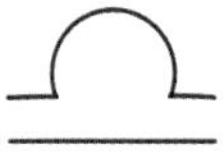

Libra
Grey
*Straight Stitch,
Back Stitch*

Scorpio
Black
Back Stitch

Sagittarius
Purple
Straight Stitch

Capricorn
Deep pink
Back Stitch

Aquarius
Teal
Back Stitch

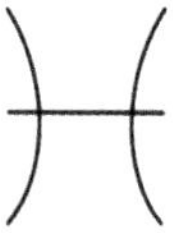

Pisces
Deep blue
Split Stitch

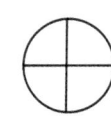

Earth
Dark green
*Straight Stitch,
Back Stitch*

Mars
Purple
*Straight Stitch,
Split Stitch*

Jupiter
Beige
Back Stitch

Saturn
Grey
*Straight Stitch,
Back Stitch*

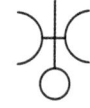

Uranus
Blue
*Scallop Stitch,
Straight Stitch*

Neptune
Deep blue
*Straight Stitch,
Stem Stitch*

Mercury
Teal
*Scallop Stitch,
Straight Stitch*

Retrograde
Black
*Straight Stitch,
Back Stitch*

'The astrology symbols can be stitched using any outline stitch that you like – you could even weave in some sparkly thread to give a more mystical feel.'

MIND, BODY, AND SPIRIT

Health

COLOURS

Yellow 972
Peach 754
Orange 946
Red 321
Burgundy 814
Deep pink 600
Pink 603
Lilac 554
Purple 552
Deep blue 798
Blue 334
Pale blue 3841
Teal 3809
Green 701
Moss green 581
Dark green 3818
Brown 898
Tan 167
Beige 739
Grey 414
White BLANC
Black 310

Syringe
White, Grey
Straight Stitch, Scallop Stitch

Heartbeat
Red
Straight Stitch

Pills
White, Deep blue
Satin Stitch

Pill Bottle
Brown, Beige
Straight Stitch, Scallop Stitch

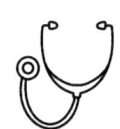

Stethoscope
Beige, Grey
Back Stitch, Whipped Back Stitch

First Aid Kit
Dark green, Red
Straight Stitch, Scallop Stitch, Satin Stitch

Plaster
Tan
Back Stitch, Straight Stitch, Seed Stitch

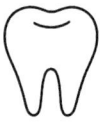

Tooth
White
Split Stitch

Thermometer
White, Yellow, Grey
Satin Stitch

Drop of Blood
Red, Beige
Satin Stitch, Scallop Stitch

Wheelchair
Black, Grey
Back Stitch, Straight Stitch, Scallop Stitch

Walking Stick
Tan, Black
Split Stitch, Satin Stitch

Ambulance
Red, White, Black, Yellow, Pale blue
Satin Stitch, Scallop Stitch, Straight Stitch

Crutches
Grey, Beige, Black
Straight Stitch, Split Stitch, Satin Stitch

Broken Bone
Beige
Satin Stitch

Face Mask
Blue, Beige
Stem Stitch, Back Stitch

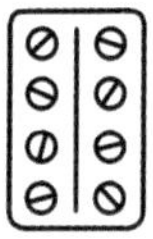

Tablets
Grey, Beige
Scallop Stitch, Straight Stitch

X-ray
Black, White
Satin Stitch, Scallop Stitch, Straight Stitch

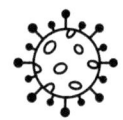

Germ
Green, Moss green
Back Stitch, French Knot, Lazy Daisy, Straight Stitch

Inhaler
Blue, Grey, Pale blue
Satin Stitch, Straight Stitch

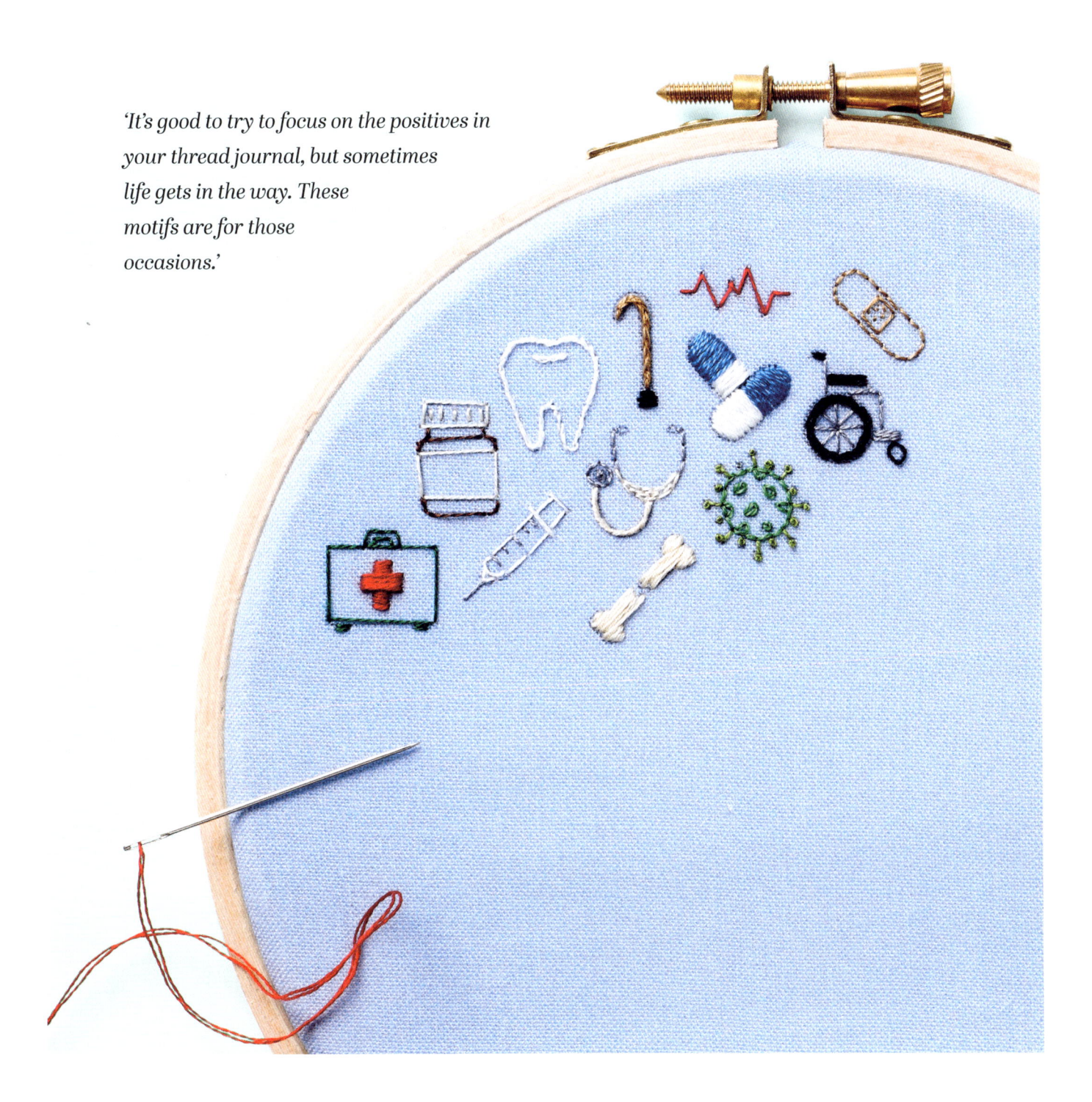

'It's good to try to focus on the positives in your thread journal, but sometimes life gets in the way. These motifs are for those occasions.'

ASTRONOMY

Space

COLOURS

Yellow 972
Peach 754
Orange 946
Red 321
Burgundy 814
Deep pink 600
Pink 603
Lilac 554
Purple 552
Deep blue 798
Blue 334
Pale blue 3841
Teal 3809
Green 701
Moss green 581
Dark green 3818
Brown 898
Tan 167
Beige 739
Grey 414
White BLANC
Black 310

Moon
Beige
Back Stitch, Scallop Stitch, French Knot

Satellite Dish
Grey, White
Satin Stitch, Straight Stitch, French Knot

Waxing Crescent
Black, Beige
Satin Stitch

Waning Crescent
Black, Beige
Satin Stitch

Third Quarter
Black, Beige
Satin Stitch

Astronaut Helmet
White, Black, Grey
Satin Stitch, Straight Stitch, Back Stitch

Spaceship
Pale blue, Deep blue, Orange
Back Stitch, French Knot

Crescent Moon
Beige
Satin Stitch

Moon and Cloud
Yellow, White
Satin Stitch, French Knot

Mars
Red, Orange
Satin Stitch

Saturn
Beige, Tan
Back Stitch

Earth
Moss green, Deep blue
Back Stitch

Star
Yellow
Satin Stitch

Star Cluster
Yellow
Satin Stitch, French Knot

Shooting Star
Yellow, Pale blue
Back Stitch

Satellite
Pale blue, Deep blue
Straight Stitch, Scallop Stitch

Fireball
Red, Orange, Yellow
Back Stitch, Straight Stitch

Rocket
Red, White, Yellow
Straight Stitch, Scallop Stitch

Galaxy
Pale blue, Yellow
Back Stitch, French Knot, Scallop Stitch

Telescope
Black
Straight Stitch

'You can make these space-themed designs as complex or as simple as you feel comfortable with. You can either try outlining the designs or filling them in with Satin Stitch or French knots, for example.'

GENRE

Fantasy

COLOURS

Yellow 972
Peach 754
Orange 946
Red 321
Burgundy 814
Deep pink 600
Pink 603
Lilac 554
Purple 552
Deep blue 798
Blue 334
Pale blue 3841
Teal 3809
Green 701
Moss green 581
Dark green 3818
Brown 898
Tan 167
Beige 739
Grey 414
White BLANC
Black 310

Unicorn
Pale blue, Pink, Lilac, Blue, Black
Scallop Stitch, Straight Stitch, Satin Stitch

Pegasus
White, Grey, Black
Stem Stitch, Straight Stitch, Scallop Stitch, French Knot

Fairy
Lilac, Pale blue, Yellow, Peach
Satin Stitch, Scallop Stitch, Back Stitch

Gnome
Red, Beige, Brown, Peach
Satin Stitch, French Knot

Toadstool House
Red, Brown, Beige
Back Stitch, Straight Stitch, French Knot

Bigfoot
Tan, Brown
Scallop Stitch, Straight Stitch

Cyclops
Moss green, Pale blue, Black, Yellow
Back Stitch, Scallop Stitch, French Knot, Satin Stitch

Phoenix
Red, Orange
Satin Stitch

Loch Ness Monster
Green, Teal, Black
Scallop Stitch, French Knot, Back Stitch

Castle
Pale blue, Pink
Straight Stitch, Scallop Stitch, Satin Stitch

Mermaid
Green, Tan, Orange
Scallop Stitch, Back Stitch, French Knot

Genie
Purple, Pale blue, Peach, Yellow
Scallop Stitch, French Knot

Wand
Pale blue, Yellow
Straight Stitch, Satin Stitch, Seed Stitch

Shield
Dark green, Burgundy, Grey
Satin Stitch, Split Stitch

Cauldron
Black, Grey, Moss green, Green
Satin Stitch, French Knot, Scallop Stitch

Treasure Chest
Brown, Yellow, Tan, Red
Straight Stitch, Scallop Stitch, French Knot

Dragon
Dark green, Red
Scallop Stitch, Back Stitch, French Knot

Crystal Ball
Pale blue, Teal, Yellow, Tan
Back Stitch, Scallop Stitch, Straight Stitch

Sword
Grey, Yellow, Burgundy
Straight Stitch, Satin Stitch

Werewolf
Grey, Black, Yellow, White
Scallop Stitch, Satin Stitch, Straight Stitch

'These fantasy motifs are really fun to stitch. You could customise them to represent a good movie you've seen or book you've read.'

COMMUNICATION

Symbols

COLOURS

Yellow 972
Peach 754
Orange 946
Red 321
Burgundy 814
Deep pink 600
Pink 603
Lilac 554
Purple 552
Deep blue 798
Blue 334
Pale blue 3841
Teal 3809
Green 701
Moss green 581
Dark green 3818
Brown 898
Tan 167
Beige 739
Grey 414
White BLANC
Black 310

Time
Tan, Pale blue, Brown
*Satin Stitch,
Back Stitch*

Lock
Tan, Black, Grey
*Satin Stitch, Straight
Stitch, Stem Stitch*

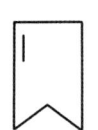

Bookmark
Red
Straight Stitch

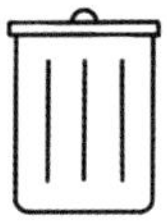

Bin
Grey
*Back Stitch, Straight
Stitch, Scallop Stitch*

Magnifying Glass
Grey, Black
*Satin Stitch,
Split Stitch*

Stop / No
Red
Stem Stitch

Pride Flag
Red, Orange, Yellow, Green,
Blue, Purple, Black, Brown,
Pale blue, Pink, White
Satin Stitch

Hashtag
Black
Satin Stitch

Recycle
Dark green
Satin Stitch

Bell
Yellow, Tan, Pale blue
*Satin Stitch,
Scallop Stitch*

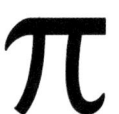

Pi
Black
Split Stitch

White Flag (Surrender)
White, Tan
*Satin Stitch,
Straight Stitch*

Law
Tan, Brown
*Straight Stitch, Scallop
Stitch, French Knot*

Peace
Deep blue
Back Stitch

Infinity
Black
Split Stitch

Light Bulb (Idea)
Yellow, Grey
*Straight Stitch, Back
Stitch, Scallop Stitch*

Semicolon
Black
Satin Stitch

Warning
Black, Red
*Split Stitch, Satin Stitch,
French Knot*

Shopping
Grey, Black
*Straight Stitch,
Scallop Stitch*

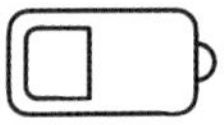

Battery
Red, Grey
*Satin Stitch, Back Stitch,
Scallop Stitch*

'The warning sign symbol is stitched using four strands of red to give the triangle a bold look. You can stitch it using just two strands if you don't want it to stand out as much.'

COMMUNICATION

Doodles

COLOURS

Yellow 972
Peach 754
Orange 946
Red 321
Burgundy 814
Deep pink 600
Pink 603
Lilac 554
Purple 552
Deep blue 798
Blue 334
Pale blue 3841
Teal 3809
Green 701
Moss green 581
Dark green 3818
Brown 898
Tan 167
Beige 739
Grey 414
White BLANC
Black 310

Heart
Deep pink, Pink
Satin Stitch, Seed Stitch

Star
Yellow
Straight Stitch

Flower
Purple, Lilac
Split Stitch, Satin Stitch

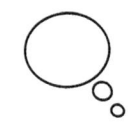

Thought Bubble
Blue
Back Stitch, Scallop Stitch

Speech Bubble
Black
Split Stitch

Question Mark
Red
Back Stitch, Scallop Stitch

Exclamation Mark
Orange
Satin Stitch

3D Heart
Pink
Back Stitch

Ditsy Daisies
Lilac, Pink, Purple
Scallop Stitch

Chunky Arrow
Green
Satin Stitch

Paper Aeroplane
Grey
Straight Stitch

Sunshine
Yellow
Satin Stitch, Seed Stitch

Arrow
Deep blue
Straight Stitch

Idea Bubble
Teal
Scallop Stitch

Moon and Star
Pale blue, Yellow
Satin Stitch

Shooting Star
Yellow, Pink, Purple
Satin Stitch, Back Stitch

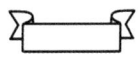

Banner
White
Straight Stitch, Scallop Stitch

Tulip
Lilac, Moss green
Satin Stitch, Straight Stitch, Scallop Stitch

Lightning
Yellow
Straight Stitch

Cloud
Blue, Black
Scallop Stitch

'These doodle designs are great if you're stuck for an entry for your thread journal. They stitch up super quickly and add a nice pop of colour!'

COMMUNICATION

Emojis

COLOURS

Yellow 972
Peach 754
Orange 946
Red 321
Burgundy 814
Deep pink 600
Pink 603
Lilac 554
Purple 552
Deep blue 798
Blue 334
Pale blue 3841
Teal 3809
Green 701
Moss green 581
Dark green 3818
Brown 898
Tan 167
Beige 739
Grey 414
White BLANC
Black 310

In Love
Yellow, Red, Black
Satin Stitch

Laughing
Yellow, White, Red, Black
Satin Stitch, Back Stitch

Winking
Yellow, Pink, Black
Satin Stitch, Scallop Stitch, French Knot

Sunglasses
Yellow, Black
Stem Stitch, Satin Stitch, Scallop Stitch

Dead
Yellow, Black
Satin Stitch, Cross Stitch

Eye Roll
Yellow, Black
Satin Stitch, French Knot, Straight Stitch

Shocked
Yellow, Black
Satin Stitch, French Knot

Angry
Yellow, Orange, Red, Black
Satin Stitch, Scallop Stitch, Straight Stitch

Poo
Brown, Black, Tan
Satin Stitch, French Knot, Straight Stitch

Fire
Red, Yellow
Satin Stitch

Crying Laughing
Yellow, Blue, Black
Split Stitch, Scallop Stitch, Satin Stitch

Sad
Yellow, Black, Blue
Stem Stitch, Scallop Stitch, Satin Stitch

Loved
Yellow, Red, Black
Split Stitch, Satin Stitch, Scallop Stitch

Disappointed
Yellow, Black, Blue
Back Stitch, Satin Stitch, Scallop Stitch

Happy
Yellow, Pink, Black
Satin Stitch, French Knot, Scallop Stitch, Back Stitch

Praying
Peach, Deep blue
Straight Stitch, Scallop Stitch

Thumbs Up
Tan
Back Stitch, Scallop Stitch

Heart
Red, White
Satin Stitch, Scallop Stitch

Twinkle
Yellow
Satin Stitch

Eyes
Black
Satin Stitch, Back Stitch

120

'The angry emoji is stitched using a gradient of red, orange and yellow. You can achieve this by satin-stitching a block of each colour and then using a single strand of orange thread to blend in where the colours join with Straight Stitch.'

COMMUNICATION

Alphabet, Numbers and Diacritics

COLOURS							
Yellow 972	*Aa*	*Bb*	*Cc*	*Dd*	*Ee*	*Ff*	*Gg*
Peach 754	Aa	Bb	Cc	Dd	Ee	Ff	Gg
Orange 946							
Red 321							
Burgundy 814							
Deep pink 600	*Hh*	*Ii*	*Jj*	*Kk*	*Ll*	*Mm*	*Nn*
Pink 603	Hh	Ii	Jj	Kk	Ll	Mm	Nn
Lilac 554							
Purple 552							
Deep blue 798							
Blue 334							
Pale blue 3841	*Oo*	*Pp*	*Qq*	*Rr*	*Ss*	*Tt*	*Uu*
Teal 3809	Oo	Pp	Qq	Rr	Ss	Tt	Uu
Green 701							
Moss green 581							
Dark green 3818							
Brown 898							
Tan 167	*Vv*	*Ww*	*Xx*	*Yy*	*Zz*	?	!
Beige 739	Vv	Ww	Xx	Yy	Zz	? Question mark	! Exclamation mark
Grey 414							
White BLANC							
Black 310							

122

COMMUNICATION

'If you're stitching a word, remember to reduce the size of the characters so they don't take up too much space on your journal.'

'Happy Birthday!'

'Happy Birthday!'

'You can add the months of the year, a name or a special date to your journal.'

0	1	2	3	4	5	6	7	8	9
Zero	One	Two	Three	Four	Five	Six	Seven	Eight	Nine

+	−	×	=	%	#	@	/ \	_	*
Plus	Minus	Multiply	Equal	Percentage	Hash	At symbol	Forward slash, backslash	Underscore	Asterisk

< >	§	$	£	€	¥	æ œ	ß	, .	: ;
Less than, greater than	Section/micro	Dollar	Pound	Euro	Yen	Ligatures	Eszett (e.g.: Straße)	Comma, full stop	Colon, semicolon

" "	'	&	( )	{ }	[ ]	´ `	^ ˇ	~ ¨	° ¸
Double quotes	Apostrophe/ single quotes	Ampersand	Open/closing parenthesis	Open/closing curly bracket	Open/closing square bracket	Acute accent (e.g.: café), grave accent (e.g.: crème)	Circumflex (e.g.: côte), háček (e.g.: kuře), breve (e.g.: kŭt)	Tilde (e.g.: piñata), diaeresis or umlaut (e.g.: Noël)	Degree/Angstrom (e.g.: åtta), cedilla (e.g.: façade)

Index

A
Abacus 104
Acorn 38
Acoustic Guitar 86
Aeroplane 8, 76
Aeroplane Window 76
Alligator 26
All-Seeing Eye 106
Aloe Vera 44
Alphabet 122
Ambulance 110
American Football 78
American Football Helmet 78
Analogue Watch 100
Anchor 76
Angel 72
Angry Emoji 120
Ant 32
Anteater 28
Anthurium 40
Apple 54
Apron 48
Aquarius 108
Archery Target 80
Aries 108
Arrow 118
Ash Leaves 38
Astronaut Helmet 112
Aubergine 54
Avocado 54
Axe 88

B
Baby Bath 102
Baby Face with Bow 102
Baby Face with Dummy 102
Babygrow 102
Backpack 76, 88
Bacon 18, 50
Badminton Shuttlecock 78
Bag of Crisps 50
Bag of Wheat 24
Bagel 50
Baked Potato 50
Ballet Shoes 80
Balloon 66
Balloon Dog 66
Banana 20, 54, 60
Banana Split 58
Banner 118
Bare Tree 38
Barn 24
Barn Owl 30
Barrel Cactus 44
Baseball Bat and Ball 78
Baseball Cap 100
Basketball 78
Basketball Hoop 78
Bat 70
Battenburg 58
Battery 116
Bauble 72
BBQ 88
Beach Ball 90
Beach Hut 90
Beach Mat 90
Bear 102
Bear Rattle 102
Bear with Heart 68
Bee 32
Beech leaf 38
Beer 56
Beetle 32
Bell 72, 116
Belt 100
Bib 102
Bicycle 76
Bigfoot 114
Bin 116
Binoculars 84, 88
Birdcage 34
Birdhouse 64
Birds 90
Birthday Cake 66
Birthday Card 66
Black Cat 70
Blazer 98
Blossom 40
Blouse 98
Blow Dryer 96
Blue Jay 30
Blue Whale 36
Bobbin 84
Bobble Hat 100
Boiled Sweet in Wrapper 60
Boiled Egg 50
Bone 34
Bongo 86
Book 84
Bookmark 116
Boot 46, 100
Bottle 102
Bottle of Pop 56
Bouquet 62
Bow 66, 100
Bow and Arrow 68
Bowl of Soup 50
Bowling Ball and Pin 78
Box of Chocolates 68
Boxing Glove 80
Bra 98
Bride 62
Briefcase 94
Briefs 98
Broccoli 54
Broken Bone 110
Broken Heart 68
Brontosaurus 26
Bucket 90
Bucket Hat 100
Budgie 34
Building Blocks 104
Bull Face 24
Bullrush 38
Bunch of Balloons 66
Bunny 64
Bunny Ear Cactus 44
Bunting 66
Burger 52
Butterfly (1) 32
Butterfly (2) 32
Buttons 84

C
Cabbage 54
Cake on Stand 58
Cake Slice 58
Calathea 44
Calculator 94
Calla Lily 40
Camel 28
Camera 84
Campervan 76
Campfire 21, 88
Cancer 108
Candle 62, 66, 106
Candy Cane 72
Candy Corn 9, 70
Cannon 92
Canoe 88
Capricorn 108
Capybara 28
Car 76
Carabiner 88
Card 68
Cardigan 98
Carousel 92
Carrot 54
Cassette Tape 86
Cast Iron Plant 44
Castle 114
Cat 34
Cat Face 34
Caterpillar 32
Cauldron 114
Chameleon 26
Champagne 62
Champagne Flute 56
Cheese 50
Chef's Hat 48
Cherries 54, 60
Chess Piece 84
Chestnut Leaves 38
Chick 64
Chick with Shell 64
Chicken 24
Chilli 54
Chinese Lantern 74
Chocolate 60
Chocolate Bar 60
Chopping Board 48
Christmas Light 72
Christmas Tree 72
Chunky Arrow 118
Church 62
Churros 58
Cinema Ticket 92
Circus Tent 92
Clapper Board 92
Clinking Glasses 62
Clipboard 94
Clippers 96
Clock 94
Cloud 118
Clown 66
Clown Fish 36
Coat 98
Cobra 26
Cockle Shell 90
Cocktail 56
Coffee Beans 56
Coffee Pot 56
Coffin 70
Coiled Shell 90
Cola Bottle 60
Collar 34
Comb 96
Compact 96
Compass 88, 94
Compost 46
Computer Monitor 94
Concert 92
Confetti 62
Cookie 58
Cooking 82
Coral 36
Corn Dog 52
Cow 24
Cow Face 24
Crab 36
Cracker 72
Crescent Moon 112
Crescent Moon and Star 74
Crib 102
Cricket 78
Crochet Hook 82
Crocodile 26
Crocus 40
Croissant 50
Cross Stitch 19, 82
Crossbones 70
Crossword 84
Crown 66
Crucifix 74
Crutches 110

INDEX

Crying Laughing Emoji 120
Crystal Ball 114
Crystal Wand 106
Cupcake 58
Cupcake with Cherry 58
Curling Wand 96
Cyclops 114

D

Daffodil 40
Dahlia 40
Dahlia in Vase 44
Daisies 44
Daisy 7, 40
Dandelion 38, 40
Dart Board 82
Dead Emoji 120
Decorated Tree 72
Desert Cactus 44
Dharma Wheel 74
Diacritics 123
Dice 84
Digital Watch 100
Dino 104
Direction Sign 76
Disappointed Emoji 120
Disco Ball 92
Ditsy Daisies 118
Diyas (Diwali Candle) 74
Dog 34
Dog Face 34
Dollar 123
Dolly 104
Dolphin 36
Dominoes 82
Doughnut 58
Door Hanger 62
Dove 62
Dragon 114
Dragonfly 32
Dress 98
Drill 46
Drop of Blood 110
Drum 86
Duck 30
Duckling 64
Duffel Bag 100
Dummy 102

E

Eagle 30
Earrings 100

Earth 108, 112
Easel 82
Easter Bunny 64
Easter Egg 64
Easter Egg (2) 64
Easter Tree 64
Easter Wreath 64
Eerie Moon 70
Egg Hunt Sign 64
Egg with Bow 64
Egg with Butterfly 64
Eggs 64
Eggs in Basket 64
Electric Guitar 86
Elephant 28
Email 94
Engagement Ring 62
Envelope 68
Euro 123
Evening Dress 98
Evil Eye 106
Exclamation Mark 118, 122
Eye Roll Emoji 120
Eyeball 70
Eyebrow 96
Eyelashes 96
Eyes Emoji 120
Eyeshadow 96

F

Face Cream 96
Face Mask 110
Fairy 114
Falling Leaves 38
Fangs 70
Farfalle Pasta 52
Farmer's Hat 24
Fencing 80
Ferris Wheel 92
Fidget Spinner 104
Fields 24
Film 92
Fir 72
Fir Tree 38
Fire Emoji 120
Fireball 112
Fireworks 74
First Aid Kit 110
Fish 36
Fish Skeleton 34
Flamingo 6, 30
Flash Drive 94

Flask 88
Flip-flops 90
Flower 118
Flower Bouquet 68
Flowers in Vase 44
Flute 86
Fly 32
Flying Heart 68
Football 78
Football Goal 78
Footprints 26, 102
Forest 88
Forget-me-Not 40
Fork and Spoon 102
Four-leaf Clover 74
Frankenstein's Monster 70
French Fries 52
Fried Egg 50
Fuchsia 40

G

Galaxy 112
Gaming Controller 92
Garden Fork 46
Gecko 26
Gemini 108
Genie 114
Germ 110
Ghost 70
Gift 72
Gift Bag 66
Gifts 66
Gilet 98
Gingerbread Man 72
Giraffe 28
Glass of Pop 56
Glasses 100
Globe 76
Glue Gun 84
Gnome 114
Goat Face 24
Goldfish Bowl 34
Golf Club and Ball 78
Goose 24
Gorilla 28
Graduation Cap 94
Grapes 54
Grasshopper 32
Grave 70
Great Tit 30
Groom 62
Gumball Machine 21, 60

Gummy Bear 60
Gymnastics 20, 80

H

Hair Scissors 96
Hair Straighteners 96
Hammer 46
Hamsa Hand 74
Hamster 34
Handbag 100
Hanging Basket with Flowers 44
Happy Emoji 120
Happy Birthday 123
Hashtag 116
Hatching Chick 64
Hatching Egg 26
Headphones 86
Headset 94
Heart 68, 118, 120
Heart and Arrow 68
Heart Balloon 68
Heart Sign 62
Heart Tag 68
Heartbeat 110
Helmet 80
Hershey's Kiss 60
Hibiscus 40
High-heeled Shoe 100
Hiking Boot 88
Hippo Face 28
Hockey 78
Holly 72
Hoodie 98
Horse 24
Horse Face 24
Hot Air Balloon 76
Hot Chocolate 56
Hot Cross Bun 64
Hot Drink 56
Hotdog 52
Hummingbird 30
Hydrangea 40

I

Ice Cream 90
Ice Cream Sundae 58
Ice Lolly 90
Ice Skate 80
Iced Bun 58
Ichthys symbol 74
Idea Bubble 118

In Love Emoji 120
Infinity 116
Inhaler 110
Interlocking bricks 104

J

Jam 50
Jelly Baby 60
Jellybean 60
Jellyfish 36
Jigsaw Piece 84
Jug 48
Jug of Flowers 64
Jupiter 108

K

Kangaroo 28
Karate 80
Kebab 52
Kennel 34
Kettle 48
Key 68
Keyboard 86
Khanda 74
Killer Whale 36
Kingfisher 30
Kite 84
Kiwi 54
Knife 48
Knitting Needles 82
Koala 28
Komodo Dragon 26

L

La Tomatina 74
Labrador 34
Ladder 46
Ladybird 32
Lamb 24, 64
Lamp 88, 94
Laptop 94
Latte 56
Laughing Emoji 120
Laurel 38
Lavender 40
Law 116
Lawn Mower 46
Leash 34
Leggings 98
Lemon 18, 54
Lemur 28
Leo 108

INDEX

Libra 108
Liquorice Allsort 60
Liquorice Allsort (2) 60
Ligatures 123
Light Bulb (Idea) 116
Lightning 42, 118
Lightning Cloud 42
Lion 28
Lips 68
Lipstick 96
Lizard 26
Loaf of Bread 50
Lobster 36
Location Symbol 76
Loch Ness Monster 114
Lock 68, 116
Log 38
Lollipop 60
Lollipop (2) 60
Long Balloon 66
Lotus 106
Love Heart 60
Love Letter 68
Love Potion 68
Love Speech Bubble 68
Loved Emoji 120
Luggage Tag 76

M

Macaron 58
Magic Wand 92
Magician's Hat 92
Magnifying Glass 116
Magnolia 40
Magpie 30
Make-up Brush 96
Mandala (1) 106
Mandala (2) 106
Mannequin 84
Map 76, 88
Maple Leaf 38
Maraca 86
Mars 108, 112
Marshmallow 60, 88
Marshmallow (2) 60
Martini 56
Mascara 96
Meat Joint 52
Meatloaf 52
Medal 80
Meerkat 28
Menorah 74

Mercury 108
Meringue 58
Mermaid 114
Microphone 86
Microwave 48
Mirror 96
Mistletoe 72
Mittens 100
Mixer 48
Mixing Bowl 48
Mobile 102
Monkey 28
Monstera Leaf 44
Monsters 44
Moon 112
Moon and Cloud 112
Moon and Star 19, 118
Moped 76
Moses Basket 102
Mosque 74
Mosquito 32
Moth 32
Mountains 88
Mouse 94
Movie Camera 92
Muffin 58
Muffin Tin 48
Mummy 70
Museum 82
Mushroom 38
Music Notes 86
Musical Hearts 62

N

Nail 96
Nail Polish 96
Nappy 102
Natural Crystal 106
Needle 82
Neptune 108
Nest 38
Newspaper 82
Notepad 94
Numbers 123

O

Oak 38
Octopus 36
Olives 52
Om 74
Om Hand 106
Onion 54

Open Book 84
Orange 54
Orangutan Face 28
Oreo 58
Origami 84
Oscar 92
Ostrich 30
Oven 48
Oven Glove 48
Oyster 36

P

Paint Palette 82
Paint Roller 46
Paint Tube 82
Paintbrush 82
Painting 82
Palm Reading 17, 106
Palm Tree 90
Pancakes 50
Panda 28
Pansy 40
Panther 28
Paper Aeroplane 118
Paperclip 94
Partridge 30
Party Blower 66
Party Hat 66
Party Popper 66
Passport 76
Pasty 50
Paw Print 88
Paw Prints 34
Peace 116
Pear 54
Pearl Necklace 100
Pegasus 114
Pelican 30
Pen 94
Pencil 82
Penguin 30
Pepper 54
Perfume 96
Pet Carrier 34
Pet Food 34
Phoenix 114
Phone 94
Pi 116
Piano 86
Picket Fence 46
Pig 24
Pig Face 24

Pigeon 30
Pilea 44
Pilgrim Hat (Thanksgiving) 74
Pill Bottle 110
Pills 110
Pin Cushion 84
Ping Pong 78
Pinwheel 104
Piping Bag 48
Pisces 108
Pizza 9, 52
Pizza Cutter 48
Pizza Oven 48
Plaice 36
Plaster 110
Playdough 104
Playing Cards 84
Pliers 46
Polar Bear 28
Polo Shirt 98
Poo Emoji 120
Poodle 34
Popcorn and Drink 92
Poppy (Remembrance) /4
Porridge 50
Potato 54
Pottery Wheel 82
Pound 123
Pram 102
Prayer Mat 74
Praying Emoji 120
Present 66
Pretzel 50
Pride Flag 116
Printer 94
Profiteroles 58
Pterodactyl 26
Puffin 30
Pull-along Dog 104
Pumpkin 7, 70
Punctuation 123
Pushchair 102

Q

Question Mark 118, 122

R

Rabbit 34
Radio 86
Rain Cloud 42
Rain Cloud (2) 42
Rainbow 42

Rainbow with Clouds 13, 42
Raindrops 21, 42
Rattle 102
Rattlesnake 26
Ray 36
Record Player 86
Recycle 116
Red Wine 56
Retrograde 108
Rhino 28
Ribs 52
Ring Stacker 104
Roast Chicken 52
Robin 30
Robot 104
Rock Balancing 106
Rocket 112
Rocking Horse 104
Rollerblade 80
Rolling Pin 48
Rosary Beads 74
Rose 40, 68
Round Brush 96
Round Cactus 44
Rowing 80
Rubber Plant 44
Ruby 106
Rudolph 72
Rugby Ball 78
Rugby Posts 78
Ruler 94
Running Shoe 80

S

Sad Emoji 120
Safety Pin 102
Sagittarius 108
Salad 52
Salami 50
Salmon 52
Sandcastle 90
Sandwich 50
Santa Hat 72
Satellite 112
Satellite Dish 112
Saturn 108, 112
Saucepan 48
Sausage 50
Sausage Roll 52
Save the Date 62
Saw 46
Saxophone 86

INDEX

Scales 48
Scarecrow 24
Scarf 100
Scissors 84
Scooter 104
Scorpio 108
Screw 46
Screwdriver 46
Scroll / Certificate 94
Seagull 30
Seahorse 36
Seal 36
Semicolon 116
Seven Chakras 106
Sewing Machine 84
Shaper Sorter 104
Shark Fin 36
Shears 46
Sheep 24
Sheep Face 24
Shell 90
Shield 114
Shield Bug 32
Shinto 74
Ship 76
Shirt 98
Shocked Emoji 120
Shoot 38
Shooting Star 112, 118
Shopping 116
Shorts 98
Shrimp 36
Simple Flower 40
Simple Tree 38
Sippy Cup 102
Skateboard 80
Skiing 80
Skipping Rope 104
Skirt 98
Skull 70
Sleeping Bag 88
Sleeping Cat 34
Slice of Bread 50
Slice of Cake 66
Slice of Pie (Egg Custard) 58
Slot Machine 92
Slug 32
Smart Shoe 100
S'more 8, 58
Smudging Stick 106
Snail 32
Snake 26

Snake Plant 44
Sneaker 100
Snooker Balls 78
Snorkel 90
Snow Cloud 42
Snow Globe 72
Snowflake 72
Snowflakes 42
Snowman 42
Socks 98
Softball 78
Spaceship 112
Spade 46, 90
Spaghetti 52
Spanner 46
Speaker 86
Speech Bubble 118
Spider 32, 70
Spider Web 70
Spinning Top 104
Spirit Glass 56
Spooky Eyes 70
Spring Flowers 64
Squid 36
Star 72, 112, 118
Star Balloon 66
Star Cluster 112
Starfish 90
Star of David 74
Steak 52
Stegosaurus 26
Stethoscope 110
Stick Insect 32
Stocking 72
Stop / No 116
Strawberry 6, 19, 54
Streamers 66
String of Pearls 44
Striped Lizard 26
Sudoku 82
Sun 42
Sun and Cloud 42, 90
Sun Behind Cloud 42
Sun Hat 100
Sunflower 40
Sunglasses 90, 120
Sunshine 118
Surfboard 80
Sushi 52
Swallow 30
Swan 30
Sweater 20, 98

Sweetcorn 54
Sweets 70
Swimming 80
Swiss Army Knife 88
Sword 114
Symbols 123
Syringe 110

T
Tablets 110
Taco 52
Takeaway Coffee 56
Takeaway Drink 56
Takeaway Noodles 52
Tall Glass 56
Tap 46
Tape Measure 84
Tarot Cards 106
Tart 58
Taurus 108
Tea 56
Tea Bag 56
Teapot 56
Telescope 112
Tennis Ball 78
Tennis Racket 78
Tent 88
Texting 82
Theatre Masks 92
Theatre Stage 92
Thermometer 42, 110
Thimble 84
Third Quarter 112
Thought Bubble 118
Three Cacti Tray 44
Three Crystals 106
Three Hearts 68
Three Mushrooms 38
3D Glasses 92
3D Heart 118
Thumbs Up Emoji 120
Tie 100
Tiger 28
Time 116
Toad 26
Toadstool 38
Toadstool House 114
Toaster 48
Tooth 110
Top Hat 62
Torch 88
Tortoise 26

Toucan 30
Tractor 24
Traditional Suitcase 76
Trailing Plant in Hanging Basket 44
Train 76
Treasure Chest 114
Treble Clef 86
Tree 38
Tree Frog 26
Tree of Life 106
T. rex 26
Triceratops 26
Triple Goddess 106
Trophy 80
Tropical Fish 36
Trousers 98
Trowel 46
Trumpet 86
T-Shirt 98
Tube of Cream 96
Tulip 40, 118
Turtle 36
TV 92
Twinkle Emoji 120
Two Clouds 42

U
Umbrella 42, 90
Unicorn 114
Uranus 108

V
Vase with Foliage 44
Vest 98
Violin 86
Virgo 108
Volleyball 78

W
Waffle 50
Walking Stick 110
Wand 114
Waning Crescent 112
Warm Pie 58
Warning 116
Wasp 32
Water Lily 40
Water Pistol 104
Watering Can 46
Watermelon 54
Wave 90

Waxing Crescent 112
Wedding Bells 62
Wedding Cake 62
Wedding Dress 62
Wedding Invitation 62
Wedding Ring 62
Weight 80
Welly 42
Werewolf 114
Wheat 24
Wheelbarrow 46
Wheelchair 110
Wheeled Suitcase 76
Whisk 48
Whistle 80
White Flag (Surrender) 116
Wind 42
Wind Cloud 42
Wind Sock 42
Windsurfing 80
Wind-up Car 104
Wine Glass 56
Winking Emoji 120
Witch's Hat 70
Wooden Train 104
Woodlouse 32
Worm 32
Wrapped Sweet 60
Wrapped Sweet (2) 60
Wreath 72
Writing 82

X
X-Ray 110
Xylophone 86

Y
Yacht 76
Yarn 82
Yen 123
Yin Yang 18, 106
Yoga Mat 106
Yo-yo 104

Z
Zebra 28
Zombie 70

127

Author acknowledgements

I would like to thank Graham Arnold and Gemma Hadfield, as well as all my family and friends for their help and support.

Credits

With grateful thanks to DMC for providing the hoops and thread used in this book.

D·M·C
DOLLFUS MIEG & CIE
FONDÉE EN 1746